Just Breathe

Scott ~
Thanks for the
help on my commute here
to DCA ☺

God Bless

The story of one man's divorce, his courage to change and the return of his heart and soul.

Just Breathe

BRIAN NASTOVSKI

B2
squared publishing
Orlando, Florida

Published by Bsquared2, LLC

Printed in the United States of America.

All biblical quotes are taken from the New King James Version.

Original work from Ransomed Heart Ministries done by John and/or Stasi Eldredge.

My ex-wives' and past girlfriends' names are pseudonyms for identity protection.

Just Breathe: One man's divorce, courage to change and return of his heart and soul. / Brian Nastovski

ISBN-13: 978-0-9881950-0-4
ISBN-10: 0988195003

Book Cover Concept by Bita Hosseini
Book Cover Graphic By Brian Russell
Book Cover Design by Cathleen Kwas

Dedication

This book is dedicated to my children Christopher, Jason, and Hannah: gifts from God. May God watch over you and keep your hearts whole and filled with Love and Joy as He has you in the palm of His hands always. You three have shown me why life is so worth living. When I see you smile, it shows me how God has shined His love upon you during the most difficult time in our lives. I am truly sorry for what you endured for many years, but know that the healing of your hearts has started and will continue. I thank you for the way you all have grown up in this process and never once showed me a negative side during this time of separation. I have never been so proud of you three as you kept your school grades up and always remained upbeat and happy to see me. The joy you have brought me makes each and every day Father's Day. Jason, thank you for the wisdom you have given me when you told me that when I get a flat I keep on going. Those words will always and forever be etched in my heart. Hannah, thank you for the hugs and being daddy's little girl. Chris, my oldest son, thank you for understanding and not holding this situation against me and for growing up a little quicker than maybe you planned. All three of you are winners and will be great at whatever it is you choose as your path in life. Always remain strong in life, keep your faith, and never let anyone take away the joy of your day. I also want to give honor and praise to Bita. At last I have found you, and to God who has been so gracious in bringing you and I together, thank you. I will never be able to thank you enough for the design idea of the book cover and will always be grateful. You have shown me love like none other in my life and God, through me, has brought you so ever close to Him the Creator of the heavens and earth and for that I am so honored to have you in my life and be a part of that. Bita you are the Godliest women I have ever met and your passion for God is extraordinary and becoming Godlier daily. I have drawn such strength from you, Bita, and I am so blessed to have you in my life as the one God has so divinely brought to me. God is great and God has given to all of us a new life, a fresh start, and a future that has God's blessing shinning all over it. I love all of you so much and this book is in honor of all of you and dedicated to you for each day I will continue to live my life with integrity and a renewed passion for life and always look up to you, as you are the ones giving me life and the reason to live it.

My mom and sister, well what can I say, thank you is not enough. I will never forget the countless hours on the phone with you two, and thank you for your support and advice when I would use it. I couldn't have asked for a better sister and mom, I love you both very much and now you get to see what all this hard work has accomplished.

Steve and Dad, thank you for the encouragement when needed and listening to me when I asked you to. I know it wasn't easy seeing me the way I was, but I remained strong and you got to see first-hand the biggest comeback of my life and one that was able due to the strength given by you two and God Almighty.

I also want to give thanks to a few friends: Greg, Ken, and Barry. Greg, you have stuck by me through this all and for that I cannot ever thank you enough. The countless hours on the phone and also the bike as we pedaled for hundreds of miles gave me the escape needed from a world that was filled with uncertainty and negativity at the time. Greg, you have been through the hardest part of my life and will forever be remembered for what you did with and for me, and for never leaving your wingman. Thanks Ken and Barry for your continuous checking in on me during the roughest time in my life; a man needs a band of brothers and you guys were them. I thank you with all my heart.

Dave, thanks for the many mornings we met for talks during my divorce. We never stopped talking about helping Men as we always saw the need to help and find a way to get a man's heart and soul back and to bring motivation and encouragement back into his life. Always remain positive and stay encouraged my friend.

Kevin U., where do I start brother. Wow is a start—you have been a savior to me as you counseled me through the most traumatic time of my life. I can never repay you for the many hours you spent with me, but you telling me to write my story and me doing it is a start. I have learned so much from you and sir you are the kindest, most caring and gentle soft-spoken man I have ever met. You Kevin are a MAN I am inspired to be like. Your wife is blessed to have you. Always remain true to you and keep doing what you do; it makes a difference in this life.

God Bless you all, and to my kids, I love you so much and have never been more proud of you three. Stay faithful, stay strong, and I will always be there for you.

Brian Nastovski / Daddy

Acknowledgements

I want to thank the editors from Kirkus who done an amazing job and on time. You have given the book what it needed in the form of structure and grammar.

Bita Hosseini: I cannot thank you enough for coming up with the cover design based on my concept using my core message E.S.P. It was an honor and an amazing time watching it come together with you.

Brian Rusell: Thank you for bringing Bita's idea to the cover with your graphic's skill and for the work on the website.

Cathleen Kwas: Thank you for taking this book and actually giving life from a Word doc to a real book through typesetting.

All of you made my first book the best experience I could have asked for and one that I look forward to repeating with future books.

Brian Nastovski

Table of Contents

The Beginning and the End

But those who wait on the LORD shall renew their strength; they shall mount up with wings like eagles, they shall run and not be weary, they shall walk and not faint.

—ISAIAH 40:31

The sky was blue on Thursday, October 7. A light breeze blew through the open windows and the day seemed fairly normal. I placed a plate of food in the microwave and set the timer for two minutes. The vent fan whirred softly in the background, and I heard my wife Kate say, "I cannot do this anymore. I am done." Tears flowed down her cheeks as she spoke. This marked the beginning of the end of our lives together, and the start of our new separate journeys. As you read my story, focus on God and listen for His voice as He speaks to your heart. He will guide you through the process of healing and restoration. The process will be tough, but if you remain strong and stay focused, I promise you will win your life back. God has a great life planned for you.

Trust in the LORD with all your heart, and lean not on your own understanding; in all your ways acknowledge Him, and He shall direct your paths.

—PROVERBS 3:5–6

For I know the thoughts that I think toward you, says the LORD, thoughts of peace and not of evil, to give you a future and a hope.

—JEREMIAH 29:11

My world was about to change forever. I looked to Kate and asked, "You're what?" I knew what she meant, but I had entered a state of numbness and pure denial. Our marriage had lasted sixteen years and four months, and was about to end much too quickly. We were embarking on the path to become a statistic. We hadn't really argued in several months, but we hadn't really talked, either.

We had come to such a low in our relationship of almost nineteen years that when we did talk, we argued. We were roommates instead of intimate life partners, just two adults sharing a house and expenses. I had to agree with her; I was tired also. Neither of us knew how to fix our marriage.

Our inability to communicate didn't improve as we moved to separate and divorce. On the contrary, a war began. I said nasty things that wounded her, and she responded in kind. The exchanges built layers of guilt and mistrust, compounded by our lack of skill with conflict resolution. I later realized this was not God's plan for dealing with hurt and anger. I alone was responsible for my actions, and I made some poor decisions. After months of arguing and treating each other terribly, we came to the point of no return. I wasn't prepared for the emotional, physical, financial, and relational stresses caused by divorce. It was ugly.

In the early stages after I left, I was confused and spent many days in numbness, denial, and shock. I started talking to God. I asked, "Why, God? Why me?" But I now realize His truth. God used the difficulties, grief, conflict, and pain to create in me something truly great. In our darkest moments, we go to Him, and through this test of our faith, we learn to trust Him.

> *Be of good courage, and He shall strengthen your heart, all you who hope in the LORD.*
> —PSALM 31:24

> *Why are you cast down, O my soul? And why are you disquieted within me? Hope in God, for I shall yet praise him for the help of His countenance.*
> —PSALM 42:5

> *I can do all things through Christ who strengthens me.*
> —PHILIPPIANS 4:13

Through the pain, seeking God, learning how to better convey my feelings with people and deal with loss, I developed stronger perseverance, valuable character traits, and a renewed faith. I poured out my soul to God during this time in my life and felt His hand guiding me through the process. He worked His miracle in me.

A rebirth of faith came, as it had before from time to time, but this return was different. It was a revival and resurrection—I became a new creation. It began with getting myself straight with God through prayer, repentance, and forgiveness. I was on my knees every night. I cried with a repentant heart. I asked for forgiveness and for the ability to forgive Kate.

> *Look on my affliction and my pain, and forgive all my sins.*
>
> —PSALM 25:18

I began an in-depth study of the Bible. I read Christian books. I listened to praise and worship songs, and worshipped along. These helped me when I needed it most. God won back my complete trust. I surrendered my whole heart to Him, and released my problems to Him. This was a moment of despair for me. I considered myself capable and believed I should be able to handle my own life. I've since learned that my manhood is only authentic when submitted to God.

> *Have mercy on me O LORD, for I am weak; O LORD, heal me,*
> *for my bones are troubled.*
>
> —PSALM 6:2

I begged God for healing. He gave me forgiveness and tugged at my heart for repentance. Only then did my heart begin to heal and grow as God intended. I learned the crying was a huge part of the healing process. It was like flushing the past from me and replacing all my wrong beliefs with God's truth. Hardest for me was staying focused on God and remaining positive. I asked God to help me avoid negativity and to give me the ability to stand in faith. My flesh often wanted to refute comments and remarks; it was difficult. But with God all things are possible.

Positivity was one of my greatest survival weapons—it kept me sane. One morning I was drained and tired from not sleeping. I tossed and turned regularly from worry. In desperation, I decided to face myself and admit I was a mess. I could not do this alone. I needed help. I had to stop worrying about another's wrongdoings and hurtful words. I began to allow God's piercing sword to show me the truth about myself. I asked Him, "What is wrong with me? What do you want me to change?" As I started to explore, I found two different men. I also found my heart was not complete but totally broken, smashed, and scarred. I found a lifeless soul. I committed to God and myself; I had no distractions during my healing and restoration. I stayed away from alcohol, women, and anything else that could draw my attention from the task at hand. This was going to be the most important recovery of my lifetime. Setting my healing as a priority gave me focus, allowing God to work for the first time in my life. This was the best decision I've ever made.

I remember getting frustrated one day and out of anger I yelled, "You want this all? God, it's yours. Take it. Take it all. I am putting all my trust in You. I hope You will put my heart back together the way You truly desire it to be."

> *He is the Rock, His work is perfect; for all His ways are justice,*
> *a God of truth and without injustice; Righteous and upright*
> *is He.*
> —Deuteronomy 32:4

I came to realize that God is the ultimate truth. Now it was time to learn about His plans and His purpose for me. He was guiding me through this growth experience.

God opened my heart and I began to see and hear in a way I had never encountered. I embraced every new heartbeat.

I made an observation about men. We habitually maintain all kinds of things, like houses or hobbies, but we often ignore relationships with our wives and God. Many of us struggle to make time for reading the Bible and allowing God's word to change our lives.

Chapter 1

The Odds of
Success

The national average of marriages ending in divorce is an astonishing 54 percent. Our culture's regard for marriage decreases daily and has reached an all-time low. Divorce rates continue to climb and, even more depressing, the number of Christian marriages ending in divorce is at nearly same rate, 50 percent.

One county in Florida recorded 6,500 new divorce filings in 2011. Currently, one out of every two marriages ends in divorce. This is truly unacceptable. The twenty- to twenty-four-year-olds hold the fastest rising divorce rates.

For second marriages the divorce rate is 60 percent, and for third marriages the divorce rate is a ridiculous 73 percent. You may believe, after several failed relationships, a person might learn something about how to stay married. Apparently, this isn't true. Strangely, financial strain is the number-one cause in most divorces.

What is the definition of marriage? Wikipedia, a pop culture source, defines marriage as "a social union or legal contract between people that creates kinship. It is an institution in which interpersonal relationships, usually intimate and sexual, are acknowledged in a variety of ways, depending on the culture or subculture in which it is found. Such a union [is] often formalized via a wedding ceremony."

Biblically, we can point to verses: 1 Corinthians 7 (Principles of Marriage), 1 Corinthians 13 (The Greatest Gift), Ephesians 5:22–33 (Marriage—Christ and the Church), and Colossians 3:18–19.

Most people struggling through tough times in their marriage believe the grass is greener on the other side of the fence: "If only my husband/ wife were more like _____." (Fill in the blank.) We soon learn this is a fantasy and trap leading to disastrous results. Seeking happiness elsewhere is based on selfishness and denial. Marriage partners are not provided solely to offer happiness to each other. In other words, happiness does not come from your mate, but from yourself. One must first be happy and joyful in their relationship with Christ.

Tending and caring for your marriage will keep your grass green and without weeds. Many men have discovered that after jumping the fence, the original greener lawn will later turn brown due to neglect. The new lawn is soft and supple, and offers grace and mercy from a caring voice: "Come, I will console you. I will make you feel better." What seems an appealing, safe haven is only a temporary illusion filled with hurt and anguish. A broken man brings pain and anger, causing the new lawn to die. Sound familiar? In the emotional state created by a failed marriage, the last thing you need is to jump the fence. Visualize a man hopping from a pot of hot oil into a pot of cool oil sitting on a low flame. The new pot slowly heats, and before he knows it, it's just as hot as the one he jumped from. Is his situation better, worse, or the same?

This fleshly behavior causes greater pain and harm to the selfish person and those interacting with him. We get in the way of the ability to see truth. This is how it will often begin. With you reading this book, you may have already entered the divorce roller-coaster. Let me encourage you to embrace every dip and peak, and seek God's truth along the way; there will be a happy ending. There are plenty of steep climbs, fast turns, deep dips, upside-down flips, and huge emotional breakthroughs and breakdowns. The ride will cause you to feel ill at times. Grab an airsick bag, for this is a very bumpy ride!

Ephesians 6:12 says: *For we do not wrestle against flesh and blood* [contending only with physical opponents], *but against principalities, against powers, against the rulers* [the master spirits] *of the darkness of this age, against spiritual hosts of wickedness in the heavenly* [supernatural] *places.* Satan, aka the enemy, wants nothing more than for you to reside in misery. He will stop at nothing, using trickery and things that appear to be "good." As you walk the path to healing and delve deeper into God's word, the attacks may intensify. Stand strong, pursue God fervently, and you will win.

Be ready to fight for your renewed soul and heart, and avoid the enemy. Satan will slowly relinquish his grip and seek out a weaker person. Keep God in the forefront of your life. Praise and worship God, and you will prove victorious.

Chapter 2

Hometown Boy

was born in 1967 and my parents divorced when I was eighteen. Growing up in the late sixties and the seventies was different from today. I grew up in Dearborn, Michigan, a suburb of Detroit and world headquarters of the Ford Motor Corporation. Dearborn was a great town to grow up in, but today it looks more like the Middle East due to the demographic change the city went through back in the 1980s. The buildings today have Arabic writing on their signage and lots of Arabic restaurants, mosques, and pastry shops line the streets of Dearborn. The Dearborn of old was Italian pizzerias and bakeries and Polish restaurants.

I remember playing at the park near City Hall and playing army in the big field with friends. This was the time you grabbed your sword and entered into battle. We were meant to be warriors, just as God is a warrior. I always played superhero and army, anything that a boy yearned for.

My home wasn't religious, but we went to Easter Sunday Mass, as my father was Greek Orthodox and that is what I was baptized. I remember as a kid the humid summer nights and the sound of Detroit Tigers baseball on the radio at my next-door neighbor's house while sitting on the front porch enjoying iced tea. Cicada bugs chirped through the day and hard rains made my street a river and a means of cooling off. I remember the fireflies and catching them and putting them in Mason jars. I rubbed the glow on my hands at night and thought it was the coolest creation ever.

I remember raking the leaves that fell from the maple tree in our front yard, and holding on to the railing and jumping off the porch into the pile of leaves over and over again. My dad pedaled a bicycle with my brother on his shoulders and me on the handlebars, and we fell and got up and did it again. I remember the colorful fall leaves of Michigan and cider mills with the smell of warm doughnuts in the air and the cloudy, unfiltered cider we drank. Winter was a blast: snow days off school, sledding, and snowplows clearing the neighborhood streets. I played football in the street and was always interrupted by traffic coming down and someone screaming *Car!*

In my small backyard, we played basketball on the cement made uneven from the harsh Michigan winters until it was dark. We picked apples that had fallen from the apple tree in the backyard and dodged the bees as we did. Those were the years of my youth, ones filled with joy, and also days not so joyful in my teenage years.

1984

In 1984, Ronald Reagan was our nation's president, the Detroit Tigers won the World Series in Major League Baseball, and the Dow Jones average was at 1,287 points.

Unemployment was at 9.6 percent, a gallon of gas cost $1.21, and milk was $2.26 a gallon. The music of the eighties was the best. Van Halen's "Jump" was soaring, Bruce "The Boss" Springsteen's *Born in the USA* climbed the charts, and who could forget Madonna and Prince? It's funny how many of these acts are playing in 2012 and still selling out.

The years were moving fast. I was one year from high school graduation and did not know what I wanted for a career. I was busy with girlfriends and learning what love was about, or so I thought, but that was in an eighties song. I was your typical high school student, nothing too stellar, but I got by and graduated. The mideighties were filled with tension at our school as the Muslim population exploded and clashed with our ideology. This tension formed in us a racist view of the Muslim world, based on how certain Muslim students were becoming the big bullies on campus. Random fights were not uncommon; they would start in a hallway and finish with the police escorting the battlers out.

High school was also filled with fun, with our football team always one of the top teams in the state. I was in the band and played drums. It was a much-respected band in the state of Michigan. I thought about becoming a professional drummer, but it didn't happen. I attended summer band camps, and one can only imagine the times we had there.

The summers away from school were great. As fall approached I went deer hunting with my dad on cold mornings, and I also did a lot of skiing in the winter. I hold on to these good memories of growing up, the ones that showed me I was a normal kid and prepared me for what was ahead in my journey to manhood.

My early teenage years until college were filled with summer basketball games in the backyard and playing strikeout against a school wall. Yes, I got into a little trouble when I played with shoplifting. I also had my first experiences with marijuana.

I experimented with marijuana in high school but never liked it much. One afternoon I stopped my use of the drug after my dad came home looking for me. I was sleeping and he asked what was wrong. I looked at him, and he could tell I was not normal; I never slept in the afternoon unless I was sick. He almost cried, like he had emotionally failed me. I never touched the stuff after that day.

The eighties provided me with great memories: first true love, first concerts, and many other firsts. The music was some of the best. We all went through the parachute pants phase, followed by the Members Only phase, and who can forget the *Miami Vice* phase?

I had the white pants, blue shirt, and the deep tan from the tanning beds. I worked out pretty heavily, so I was looking good, I thought. My buddy Joe had a different car most weekends, and many with turbo boost in them, and the women loved it.

One year my best friend Joe and I went camping north of Detroit and met a couple girls there. It was the closest I'd come to having sex so far. We got someone to buy us a bottle of schnapps and the four of us drank it. I received the biggest hickey of my life. Pink Floyd played on the radio and we were in rock heaven. Life was good and it was the beginning of adulthood, or so I thought.

Chapter 3

The Early Wounds
of the Heart

I went through a couple really good relationships that shaped how I dealt with them, and they were also where I received my first wounds. The first one was in elementary school, and that was when I learned to chase beauty. In kindergarten, I would pretend that the wood floor was the water, the girls would be pretend swimming, and drowning and I would jump off a small balance beam to their rescue. We would also use dolls as a backup to the girls at times continuing our practice in rescue. This was the beginning of life for me as a boy learning to chase and rescue the fair maiden.

In junior high I was head over heels in love, or so I thought. Amy was the first real touch on my heart and made me feel like a man. The beginning of my manhood started there. Amy lived a few miles away and had a pretty strict dad. I remember running to her house on summer evenings while a friend paced me on his bicycle.

Asking Amy out was the hardest thing I had ever done. I was in my basement on the phone with her and had a hard time asking if she would go out with me.

I was somewhat shy growing up, and this was a huge deal. She said yes.

We attended school dances and hung out at the park, where I carved our initials on a slide. I thought, Wow, we are serious. It was the mark of a couple. I remember the perfume she wore and the color of her hair. Her parents ended our relationship because they were worried we might get involved sexually.

Their worst nightmare came true, but with her and a neighbor, not me, and she got pregnant and was never to be seen again until 1991, when I met her at a video store she worked at in Michigan. That was the first battle scar on my heart from a girl. She left me and ended up with another boy, and had a baby. Now off to another multiyear relationship: I had started college to become an aircraft mechanic, and I met a girl through my best friend at the time. That girl may have exhausted all my love and caring during my college years and sometime afterwards.

She caused another wound to my heart, but this one was the worst yet. She was my first true love, my first sexual encounter as a man. The girl that made me want to do anything for her at any time.

I was head over heels, or was I? This is why God says to wait until you're married to have sex. When we are young, it lessens the complications of a relationship by putting off the pure pleasure it is intended to give during marriage; plus, having an early family when your life is beginning is a burden.

That relationship showed me what true love meant and what it was like to wait for a woman to figure out if you're the one for her and find out you were not. It gets better, and you say, *Well, I made a mistake,* and she ends up with another man and that doesn't work out, either. More wounds for me there. I moved on and time was not graceful; it just flew by. After the early days of developing his heart and relationship skills, a man starts searching and yearning for love and his bride.

1989 and My Aviation Career

The year was 1989 and I embarked on a new career as an airline pilot. I was twenty-one years old and about to have some fun. After enjoying work as an aircraft mechanic, I decided it was time to move up. I chose the flight deck at this point in my life and never looked back. It all started in Denver, Colorado, where I went to school. I met a nice young woman who managed the hotel I stayed at for two months.

We dated while I attended classes and a little bit after that, until I moved to Las Vegas where I held my first crew base.

I was hired by Key Airlines (which is no longer in business), flying the B-727 as a flight engineer and based in Las Vegas. A flight engineer is the third person on the flight deck of most large aircraft and in charge of monitoring the aircraft's systems and maintaining optimum cabin temperature. I learned that I was first in line when women came for a quick visit to the flight deck. It was the best job on the planet. Like most twenty-one-year-olds (soon to be twenty-two), I dated very fast and enjoyed being alive. I enjoyed the beautiful women and fast-paced lifestyle until I met Brooke, who was a flight attendant with the same airline. We later married. It was the first time since my other failed relationships that I had felt love, and my future wife was absolutely beautiful. How did I get so lucky and marry this woman? We had lots in common: our jobs with the airline, love for each other, and great sex, and we laughed a lot. As the months passed, so did our passion for each other.

By this point I had started an aircraft maintenance company in Las Vegas, because I was unemployed. Key Airlines was doing poorly, and their aircraft did not require my job anymore because they were now two-pilot planes.

The stress of the few months of living poorly and fighting for what we had left would certainly prove helpful to me in my fight during my current divorce.

It is amazing how God works in ways we cannot accept at the time. Brooke and I lived in a low-income housing apartment in Las Vegas after I was laid off, paying the rent month to month, and it was something I vowed to never let happen again. I do not recall the reason for our divorce now, other than we were young and the timing was wrong, and we married for lust not love. I had another wound on my heart from an abortion during the marriage and, boy, did that hurt. Brooke felt at the time that we were not in the position to start a family and raise children due to our financial situation and how the relationship was crumbling. This was a big blow to me, and the years that followed gave me hard reminders of the day we terminated her pregnancy. I went to the clinic and waited shamefully, yet concerned for her health, and then she was let out a back door, completely drugged. I had to put her in the car and fasten the seat belt on her. I wept many times after that.

We moved back to Michigan into my mom's house after a period of time without a job. It was hard to live in the house the way we were. We moved back to Las Vegas, then to Salt Lake City for a short time for her new job. We separated and divorced shortly afterward. Another wound to the heart from a woman. I was again thrown into a feeling of failure in a relationship, only this time it was marriage. I wasn't searching for God as I would several years later, but the events in my life that were planned by God gave me the drive to seek Him after all. I turned to Tarot card readers for answers—a big mistake.

After my failed marriage, I was recalled after a furlough from Evergreen Int'l, the airline I had joined since leaving my last job.

I was flying the B-747 as a flight engineer at the age of twenty-three. I thought, *Now I am an international pilot and somebody please stop me.* Not really. I dated a girl I had worked with at my previous airline, and we connected. I felt so strongly shortly into the relationship that I got scared and pushed her away. This may sound all too familiar to some. I wasn't about to let her give me another wound, and this time it was my turn to give one.

I eventually chased after her but she stayed away, and she ended up giving me yet another wound to my heart. I wondered through the years if I had pushed my soul mate away, but I will never know, and time will erase that experience from my mind. We worked well together in most ways. We laughed, we loved, we were young, and we were good together. She was gorgeous, with an awesome body, and we clicked with everything we did. Both of us were fresh out of a divorce. I did not want my heart broken again, so instead of working on that by being the best man she could be with, I did the opposite.

How many of you can relate to this "you are not stomping on my heart" syndrome? After this girlfriend, I didn't date until I met my now ex-wife Kate.

Chapter 4

How It All Began

The year was 1993, maybe springtime, and I was eating at a bar restaurant in Kissimmee, Florida, that my friends and I frequented. A tall, brunette, and beautiful young woman caught my eye. I had to immediately fight for the right to talk with her, as my buddy was vying for her at the same time. Her name was Kate she was a schoolteacher and pretty conservative compared to the way I had been living it up the last few years. We talked and decided to meet for a drink. I had a softball game on Thursday or Friday and asked her to meet me there and go for a beer afterward. I don't recall the inning but I spotted Kate and her dog, and at that moment God changed my life forever. We chatted at the game, and I was awestruck by her beauty. Kate was about five-ten, and since I am six-two, it was great to meet a tall woman—and what a body she had.

Kate was twenty-three, fresh out of college, and teaching second grade. She was one hottie I was hot for.

The initial dates were great, and I always wanted to see her. On one occasion I waited for Kate in the parking lot while she watched a movie and brought a bottle of wine to share with her. When we first met I told Kate I worked for the Department of Sanitation, which was not true. I came clean and told Kate what I really did a few days after starting to see her. I had come out of two relationships, and it had been five or six months since I had broken up with my previous girlfriend.

I thought this new woman was it for me, but now I see differently. I had already started to sabotage my relationship with her. Kate had come out of a relationship with a man right before me, and I received only part of the story. I felt like a second fiddle at times because of her last boyfriend, but our getting closer soon displaced that. We argued a little, and that may have been the "pushing away" effect we both were dealing with.

I rented a house with a friend prior to meeting Kate. Shortly after I met Kate, the owner of the rental wasn't paying his bills and his creditors were looking for him, and I was going to be kicked out. I started living with Kate, as she was very accepting and willing to take me in. Once I moved in, relationship problems started to surface. We were two single people in control of our own lives and forced to live together, and we had to compromise and work together. She was more reserved than I was, and that presented problems.

When we met I was furloughed from the place I worked and waiting to be recalled. My job required me to be gone at three-week intervals, and then home for two weeks. She and I never got to know each other; I was either off to work or just back, and we lived around my schedule. When I returned home I wanted to party and relax a little.

She had papers to grade and I had beer to drink, and we were far apart in those aspects. She had few friends and I had many, and I wanted to see them when I returned, because they helped maintain my identity. In a way I did the same thing with my girlfriend in Las Vegas, trying to push her away, but then I would chase and she came back instead of running. Getting married a second time was scary due to my previous failures, and I was not too sure if I wanted to do that again. An odds-maker would have given me a 60 percent chance of failure.

Six to eight months passed, and it was time to ask her to marry me. No fanfare. I just asked by hiding the ring in a box of fries from a fast-food chain. Her initial reaction was NO. I wonder what was I thinking of back then; what was I afraid of? Was it that I wanted her so bad that I didn't know how to show her, or was this my pattern? What was it?

I truly thought I wanted to marry her, and I could see her as the mother of my children, but I was scared and the only way to overcome it was to jump in. How did that work for me? I ended up divorced is how. I am not saying what I did was wrong; I'm just telling what I did and the end result. If I had to do it all over again, I'm sure I would put heart, the key ingredient, into my plan of asking her to marry me. Every woman wants to be swept off her feet and have a lasting memory of the special day she was asked to be a bride. Every man is nervous on his wedding day; it's the rest of your life with this woman and that's what you say in the vows: in sickness and in health, for richer or poorer, until death do you part. What's not to be nervous about?

Pause here with me and take a moment to reflect on your current situation. Take some time to ask God to come into your heart and fill you with joy and love and grace toward your present or future wife. Ask for forgiveness and repent with a true heart for any and all wrongdoings in your life, and it will be granted. Then you can move forward.

Chapter 5

The New Beginning
and Parenthood

A fter our first son, Christopher, was born, Kate chose not to work any longer and became a stay-at-home mom. I remember the day Chris was born as if it were yesterday. I'll never forget Kate's courage. The pain got more intense with every contraction until she finally asked for an epidural.

I looked at her during labor, and she was in lots of pain. I asked her if she was okay, and she gave me a thumbs-up while lying on her right side as the anesthesiologist stuck a needle in her spine. This image of a woman with strength I have kept for many years. While Chris was being born, I held Kate's hand as we went through the breathing and pushing together. I clenched my teeth so hard during one episode that I broke part of a tooth. Pain if any was not present because of the joy of my first son being born. Then came Christopher's big entrance, and I became a dad.

Two and a half years later, Jason was born, but this time without an epidural. Jason wanted out bad, and we barely got out of the driveway before he was born. As soon as we pulled up to the hospital emergency room, I jumped out for the front door. The next thing I knew she was out of the car and in the ER. I had to move my car due to an incoming ambulance. I rushed back into the hospital, and thirty minutes later Jason entered this world. Another two years passed and we were blessed with our only girl, Hannah.

She came quickly, like Jason, and we did not know her gender until she was born. What joy when we found out she was a girl; we cried and so did the nurses. She was what we wanted, and God answered our prayers. Life changed once we started raising a family of three. We had a busy life of shuttling the children to their events. We lost focus of each other and it was noticeable. Raising a family has been fun, though very tiring at times, and very rewarding. We had the kids in private school for a few years and found it no better than public; but it did include Bible study and allowed them to speak freely about God. Children will do as well as you help them in any environment. Hannah and Jason attended a tutoring learning center and it did wonders for them. Jason was not good at math, then he turned it all around with his effort and our help through the learning center. He has since obtained a 4.0 grade average. Christopher is a gifted child; he doesn't even try and maintains a B average. When he puts in an effort, then it's a 4.0 for him also. Hannah has come a long way from being held back one year to becoming a very bright young girl.

The children have been very resilient through the divorce and maintained their grades and smiles for life. They surprised me by how they have handled my leaving the home and continued as if I was there. They have friends, school activities, and Boy Scouts, and the boys have occasional girlfriends who keep them busy. Hannah enjoys horseback riding English style and is very good at it. Horseback riding brings joy to a child, and I have seen nothing but improvement and happiness come from her weekly lessons.

When Chris was born, Kate and I took many pictures and videos of him. When Jason was born, fewer were taken, and when Hannah came, we documented very little of her life.

My life with them has been short due to my profession, and that is something I can never change. I remember the good times of raising and playing with the children as I made them laugh. I played peek-a-boo with all of them, and it made them laugh hysterically. Now we wrestle, and even Hannah gets in on the action to take her dad down.

Other times the game is for me to capture Hannah and the boys to protect or rescue her if needed. The kids have had their moments with injury but no broken bones. My wife had the responsibility of taking them to the doctor when I was flying around the world. I did see the pediatrician several times when we took the children there for various reasons. The raising of children is special; for those who get that opportunity in life, it is one that shapes you just as you shape your children.

Chapter 6

The Real Life, or
So I Thought

had the life: three kids, nice home, great job, new car, a thirty-two-foot RV—the whole package, or so I thought. In the days after my wife said she was done with our marriage, I went into great-husband mode, since I hadn't left the home yet. It was panic-driven, and I started asking her if there was anything I could do for her and told her how nice she looked, but it was too late.

It's amazing what the mind does to the emotions and the control we lose because of it. Flowers, words, and a helping hand were too late. Her reply was the same: *I'm done; this isn't working for me.*

Her shutting down and turning her heart into ice was apparent from how she spoke with me and refused to reason with me on the phone. The emotions I got from her were the coldest I have ever experienced, but I understood that this was her way of blocking any pain she felt, to keep on track and not let me derail her.

Two days later after Kate said I am done, on another beautiful October afternoon, I sensed that God began breathing new life into me.

He smiled rays of sunshine and blew the breath of life via the wind into me.

I look back on that moment, and it felt like a full-body cleanse, yet I was very scared of what I should do next, and the Father Almighty said, "My son, all will be okay. I have your back, so please trust in Me."

That same afternoon, Kate was planting a new landscape around the hot tub patio we had recently installed. My profession as a pilot has allowed me to provide a very comfortable lifestyle for Kate and the kids and some luxury items as well. As I watched Kate plant and the cable guy try to fix a re occurring problem in the backyard I began to feel very numb, as I knew what I had to do, and my stomach was in knots. It felt like I had caffeine shakes as I allowed the anxiety of the moment take me over. I knew I had to leave and never come back; I wasn't about to play the game of "This is my house and I am staying," or leave and return and live there, confusing the children. Instead, I would leave and never sleep there again; it was a matter of "I am in or out, with no in-between." The seventeen years we lived there were a big part of my life. We raised three kids, had parties with friends on occasion, and now it was going to disappear and become a place to pick up and drop off my children.

The kids were running around the yard on that beautiful, clear October day as I packed my suitcase, such a familiar feeling in my line of work as a pilot. I put it in my truck and paced nervously and with anxiety through the house. I looked around, taking mental photos, and then went into each kid's room to smell them and look at their beds one last time before returning to the backyard.

Kate was still planting in order to stay busy; she may have been mentally preparing for me to leave and file for divorce soon after. I viewed this as her nesting behavior. I looked at her and took mental pictures, and was very sad at what I was about to do, especially after what we had created together. I got her attention and said, "I am leaving now. Good-bye." She said, "What?"

It was the moment in both our lives that the roller coaster of emotions called separation began. I called a local hotel and booked a couple of nights, and I started crying as I drove away from my home.

I almost pulled over due to the emotions rushing through me, because I knew the marriage was finished. I had left my home only once before due to our relationship going badly, and that was my doing and in my control, so it was a different feeling then. I felt like a dog on the run in the streets of the night now, hiding in dark alleys and looking for shelter. That first night in the hotel felt like it lasted for years. I did not sleep; I did nothing but cry and say, *Let's grieve now and see what the next process will be.* I don't remember much of those days due to a traumalike condition that set in. On October 11, Kate filed for divorce four days after telling me she couldn't do this anymore. She may have been planning it over several months. In divorce, women are usually the petitioners, meaning the ones to file, and men are the respondents. Eighty-five percent of the women who file for divorce or separation spend about ninety days preplanning, and husbands generally have no clue of when it's coming.

(This is based on research via the internet.)

On the day she filed, we had a somewhat animated discussion about separation, which led her to file for divorce the same day. I believed that separation was not an option; I was stubborn and said that our marriage had been bad for so many years that we either worked on making it right or we simply divorced. We then talked of splitting names from credit cards and joint accounts, which included checking and savings accounts. That was when fear became an emotion for her. Her next move was to drive to her dad's and drop off our daughter, Hannah, and then drive to the attorney's office. She felt as though I was going to take all the money and leave her penniless. In this state it would have been better for us to simmer down a bit and see what was going on.

The Scene Is Set

A couple of days later she called for me to come and get the papers regarding assets and liabilities to sign, get notarized, and return. It was moving fast, and there was no "Hey, sorry," or "Love you"; it was "I have papers for you." I went to the bank for the notarization, and after filling them out, I was in such a dazed state that I cried and could barely read the papers. I had to get a grip on myself, but it was hard.

My wife's heart appeared to blacken and fill with resentment and unforgiveness. This led to a nasty pride and selfishness toward me.

She was in the painful process of separating from me, and held me accountable for all of her problems. I learned how to deal with the emotions I had when she attacked me every time we spoke.

I'm not a psychologist, but I recognized the signs of trauma that our divorce had brought on, and wondered how she was going to remain strong in front of the children but also heal through crying when alone. Kate told me the only way for her to move forward was to erase our years of marriage, one she felt cheated out of from the beginning. By divorcing me she could put the bad behind her. Then Kate spoke of the possibility of rebuilding our friendship by dating, which could lead to remarriage with a new ring. This was her idea of success and how to deal with a major problem.

I had never heard of such a crazy idea and felt that running from a problem versus trying to fix it did no good and would destroy any chance of ever making us work. Emotional trauma messes with our minds as much as we allow it to.

Kate fell deep into becoming a very unemotional person that wanted all that she had lived with and gained over the years, but minus me. Her fear of having no finances made her speak bitterly to me. I couldn't process it at the time, because I was not thinking of stopping financial support for her and the children. Kate spoke of being paralyzed by fear of the real world and of having to fend for herself for the first time in fifteen years.

Kate was a stay-at-home mom by choice and had not been in the workplace since our first child was born. So the fear of going to work hit her pretty hard.

Kate was very worried of how she was going to interview for jobs, what to wear and how to act, and, of course, employment contacts. What I witnessed was the demise of a Christian woman. The divorce-rate percentages are high among Christian relationships, so go figure. I'm not sure where the blame for this goes, the church or us.

Now I saw a woman do all the things Christ said not to do in your heart. I could not believe the transformation she made into a woman that spoke with such a cold heart and established a wall so tall there was no ladder long enough to climb over it. She believed she had no problems and said, "I will not change" and things like "I need more money." But it was the fear of the unknown that allowed her to speak like this.

I asked her once, "What is your number?" This was in regards to money and she replied, "What?"

I said, "Yes, what's your number? How much do you want or need?" I answered for her and said, "It is more, that's your number, more. You never have enough." Looking back, I did nothing to improve the situation but reacted instinctively, and it destroyed me for the day. I let the worry of how I would survive and how much was she going to get crush me. I interpreted her demands as the value she put on her life's well-being, which in the end did not get her far. Greed will sink every ship it encounters. I am not saying she was greedy, but her emotional state allowed me to interpret her quest for life as driven by greed; in reality she was scared and wondering how she was to live and take care of the children since she depended on me for financial support.

At the time I could not figure out why she chose to wallow in self-pity instead of going back to work or change her life while she had time at home when the children were in school.

This was the hardest trial of my life and riding my bike was how I defeated my stress, lost weight, and started the uphill climb into a new life with God by my side. I still loved Kate, yet she kept kicking so hard with hurtful words that made me fall on my rear. It took a little time to get up, but then my will and real strength became stronger due to my newfound skill of perseverance. That's also when my character flourished and I got up more quickly and dusted off, and did not reply with negative words but kind, heartfelt words. I stopped falling, bent over in pain as she kicked me with her barrage of discouraging words and blaming me as the one who messed up the life we had.

I managed to keep my faith and kept reading and trusting in God's word. I listened to praise and worship music and also the Dave Matthews Band; his deep, spiritual music really struck me. I noticed how the songs allowed me to meditate and help me hear from God in ways I had never imagined. We all seek something to help us get through a divorce, and my help was God, music, and my bike. I learned it was not 100 percent my fault because it takes two in a relationship.

Then I started the painful process of pouring out my heart to her and she refusing it, then making baby steps toward her, which was an exercise in character building and perseverance that God gave me. I started taking one step forward and two steps back. The hardest thing was to stay on track and take care of her and the children while being kicked by her in conversation. Like the CEO from Starbucks said, "We all fall and what matters is how we get up."

> *My brethren, count it all joy when you fall into various trials, knowing that the testing of your faith produces patience. But*

let patience have its perfect work, that you may be perfect and complete, lacking nothing.

—JAMES 1:2–4

My friends and family said, "What the heck is the matter with you? Just move on," or as my brother said, "Put the war patch on your shoulder and move forward." But I knew in my heart what I felt for her for the first time in a long time. I had to do what was right and fight for what I believed in. We had to give it one last try because there would be no more tries afterward. I watched her go through periods of depression. Unless you have a chemical imbalance, depression can be controlled.

If you ever felt your father-in-law and you were best friends during your marriage, get ready for an immediate disconnect as he moves to protect his daughter. It's another circumstance I wasn't ready to accept and never gave any thought.

Life comes flying in with challenges very quickly during a divorce. Kate's father talked with his friend who is an attorney, and he recommended the attorney that represented Kate in the divorce. The attorney was good and I knew my wife couldn't have found her at random on the Internet. For a moment I hated my father-in-law for getting such a lawyer, but I quickly overcame it. I asked God to forgive my feelings of hate toward him and forgave him for finding the lawyer.

Chapter 7

Separation and the Healing Begins

The first week out of my house and separated from Kate was very difficult. Imagine for a moment that you are a heavy smoker and the doctor said you had to quit cold turkey. That's how I felt when I no longer called my wife or drove down my street every day. It was a habit I had for many years, and I stopped overnight.

I moved in with my father for temporary relief, but more for comfort, and to allow myself to think about what had happened. It was better than hanging out in a hotel room by myself. My world was spinning out of control and I held on for the ride. I took off from work for many weeks and started the self-examination process to make the spinning stop.

I came back to my faith and asked God for help with a problem I realized was bigger than I could handle and was a job for Him. I had no control over my life and had to surrender it to God, the way we are supposed to, and trust he would provide and heal me.

I read some books, attended counseling at my local church, and signed up with a men's Christian retreat that lasted four days. It was not your typical religious men's retreat. I came to the conclusion very early in my self-examination that I had a false self, someone who I pretended to be, that I called the poser.

I went to work to get away and acted as if I was single by drinking at bars at night. When I would return home after being on the road, and a heavy feeling overcame me as if I knew my world was going to be hell once again. I started the healing process by calling friends and family and apologizing for how I had acted in their presence over the years, and especially last year. Those months were the most traumatic in my life. It felt like my whole family had been killed in a car crash and they were gone, but they were still here. I allowed myself to go deep into depression over this; things were very unclear due to guilt. I remember my anxiety and a panic attack. One morning I went to speak with Kate shortly after I had left and wanted to say the right things; I entered the house as though I was walking on eggshells. I wanted to hold her and make all this go away but knew I couldn't. She did not look me in the eyes when I spoke to her for almost two months.

I poured my heart out to her and she wanted nothing to do with it. As I left the house that morning, I felt my heart race and knew that was a feeling I would never have again. Between being addicted to her after nineteen years together and my heart beginning to open up to love again, the panic attack came as I was leaving. I knew I was not going to get her back and that it was time to get my heart and soul back for me and my children. The hard work would pay off with someone else in my life, and one day this part would be known as the dress rehearsal for what God had planned for me. I got into my truck and pulled away crying, and on the radio was the song by Jason Gray, "I Am New." God was on to something big and I didn't even know it.

In November I wrote a letter to my wife Kate, and around that same time a friend asked if I was going crazy. A counselor from church got a hold of me and wanted to know what was going on with me based on a post I sent to a church blog for prayer.

It was then I asked myself, *What is going on here, Brian?* That was when I knew I had to snap out of it.

I had to regain my life and get strong for myself, my children, and for God. I started to reevaluate what was important to me; that is God, my children, and myself. My job came in last. I worked on getting right with God, and went home to my church and asked for help in my healing. My heart was broken more than I let on from so many wounds over the years, and I went to God's emergency room for open-heart surgery. With time and God it would mend and become the best loving, caring heart, the way God intended it to be.

Here is the letter I wrote to Kate on November 11, 2011. It's called "A Man's Journey." This shows how quickly I was healing, more than I was aware. I wrote this letter in no more than forty to forty-five minutes. Some of the words I pulled out of the book *Wild at Heart: Discovering the Secret's of a Man's Soul* by John Eldredge because they fit; the others are mine.

A Man's Journey

This is not going to be like the letters I have written to you in the past. This letter is about me this time. I want to share what I have been going through this past month without you, and fill you in on my journey to becoming a real man with soul, heart, and purpose.

I have begun a journey deep into my soul to fix my heart and find out who I am and what a man really is. Deep in a man's heart are some fundamental questions that cannot be answered at the kitchen table. I ask myself, who am I? What am I made of? What am I destined for? The answers to what's my life's mission and real purpose I have to find outside.

If you think you are who you think you are, if a man is ever to find out who he is and what he's here for, he has to take that journey for himself, and I have begun. Trust me when I say I'm scared, but it's time for a tune-up.

A man has to get his heart back. My soul longs for passion, freedom, and life. So I look at questions like what makes you come alive and what stirs your heart. This journey without a clear trail is foreign to me.

Life is hypocritical if I can't live the way it moves me. Think about that for a minute.

In the heart of a man is the desperate desire for a battle to fight, an adventure to live, and a beauty to rescue. Aggression is a part of the masculine design; we were hardwired for it. Exodus 15:3 says, *The LORD is a warrior, a man of war; the LORD is His name.* God is a warrior, and man is a warrior.

There's nothing so inspiring to a man as a beautiful woman. She will make you want to charge the castle, slay the giant, or hit a home run.

This is how I have come to see you. When I look at you, I see beauty, I see a woman I want to charge the castle for and take a few arrows from the walls as I fight to win your heart. A man wants to be a hero to the beauty. I also have found that women want to be wanted, to be a priority to someone.

I get it. I am also learning that women grow bored immediately when they are made the point. You already know your story so you want to be taken into one you don't know.

I know this is deep, but this is part of my ever-changing self, finding my soul, and changing my heart as I go through this process.

You are beautiful and don't need to be tough, efficient, and independent. You are the woman I married, the woman I had children with, the woman who is an awesome housewife, the woman who cared for me. You get the point.

You are beautiful and worth fighting for. I may have seemed hollow, but I am now heading into the uncharted regions of my soul to get my heart back and be the best man God intended me to be.

I have been to counseling weekly in Oviedo and talking with Dr. Kevin Urichko at Northland Church. He was the site minister at Lyman, which I am sure you remember. I also have been talking with Pastor Gus Davies.

Northland is our home of worship, and I have come home for help to find my true heart and get it back. I am also digging deep into my soul and get right with God. I should have done this long ago.

I have been reading *Wild at Heart: Discovering the Secret of a Man's Soul* by John Eldredge. He also wrote *Love and War: Finding the Marriage*

You've Dreamed Of with his wife, Stasi, and I have read this as well. I signed up for a men's Christian retreat based on his *Wild at Heart* with John Eldredge's Ransomed Heart Ministries. It is in February and will be four days of intense talks to get my heart right again with the Lord Almighty and myself, and find the secret of my soul. I am nervous, but excited because I know this will bring me the closest I've ever been to God, and bring my heart, mind, and soul back to me so that I may share it with the kids and whoever God has planned for me, which I pray will be *you*.

You can see this journey I am on is one of finding God, the fear of the unknown, intrigue, pain, finding a lost soul, and best of all, finding love in my heart. I will come out of this journey an awesome man, and one that will make any woman proud to call me her man. I sure hope that woman is *you*.

From my heart and soul:

You can see how fast I was healing my heart, and finding it and my soul. I learned how to be a dad again and a great one and, of course, getting stronger. I regained the confidence that I had what it takes and began my journey to finding out what a real man is, and where my heart and soul went, and this is where the men's retreat comes in.

Wild at Heart Boot Camp was the name of the retreat. Ransomed Heart is a men's ministry based in Colorado and devoted to getting the heart and soul back for a man.

It started several months ago when God called a book to me titled *Love and War* by John and Stasi Eldredge. I picked up the book and turned to a random page, and it immediately drew me in like no other book. I knew God was talking to me at that moment in my life. I read the book pretty fast. I couldn't get enough of it.

I would like to pause here for a moment and use this time to pray for the healing of your hearts.

> *Jesus, I come to you with a whole heart, one that is wounded and in need of repair, one that has been assaulted and in need of repair. I ask You, Jesus, to heal my wounds and fill me with your Holy Spirit, to fill me with life once again and allow me to feel joy. Father, I ask You to cast out any and all agreements I have made with myself that prevent me from moving forward in my healing. I ask for forgiveness and that You restore my heart the way You intended it to be.*
>
> *I ask You now, Lord, to help me move forward, help me give everything to You, all my worries, all my doubts, all my agreements, and my wounded heart, and ask that You begin today to heal me. Father, allow me to feel Your breath against my face, breathe new life into my nostrils, and fill my heart with the Holy Spirit. I ask for all of this with grace and mercy, Father, in name of Your Son, Jesus Christ. Amen.*

While attending counseling at my home church, I was asked by a senior pastor if I had read the book *Wild at Heart*. I replied that I had not. He then asked me if I knew about the author, John Eldredge. I said, sure I do, I just read his latest book, *Love and War*. He said I needed to read *Wild at Heart*. So I went to my local Christian bookstore and they had five copies, and I bought all of them intending to give them to friends. I went home and read the book as fast as I could, because I was starved for knowledge and God. The book peeled away the layers of me so I could find the truth. I ask all men to fear nothing when you begin the self-evaluation process, as it will strengthen you much more and peel away the poser. Not many men have the courage to say, *I am broken, let's fix me*, so I want to congratulate those who are eager to begin the process, and encourage those yet not ready to go for it, because you are all winners. Your journey will be filled with the unknown and some hurt, but stay tuned to yourself with perspective. The healing process will take some time, but, oh, is it worth it.

The weight lifting off your shoulders as you give all to God is so freeing and necessary. Visualize with me a one-hundred-pound sack of potatoes strapped to your back and carry this for weeks and months on end. As time progresses you continually hunch over, losing strength and starting to despair. Now let's get rid of that sack, and what happens is you feel like you are floating and each day you regain your strength. You persevere and gain self-worth until you stand straight and tall again. So you tell me, do you want to be hunched over and lose the battle, or straight and tall and win the battle for your life?

After reading *Wild at Heart*, I noticed that my heart was changing and allowing me to change for the better. I stumbled on Eldredge's website and signed up for a retreat. It was the hardest thing I had to do. The fear of the unknown and "I am a man. I am not screwed up" swelled through me.

After four attempts I completed the registration process. The note kept coming up, "You have not completed registration," and I was like, no duh. Finally I registered successfully and felt great, like I was taking charge of my life and getting my heart back. I would survive and become the best son of God that he intended me to be. I could start my journey, one that allowed me to be the best dad for my children, and husband to my wife if God chooses that for me someday.

> *Deep in the heart of every man, he longs for a battle to fight, an adventure to live, and a beauty to rescue. That is how he bears the image of God; that is what God made him to be.*
> —JOHN ELDREDGE'S *WILD AT HEART*

Chapter 8

Marriage

And the LORD God said, "It is not good that man should be alone. I will make him a helper comparable for him."

So the LORD God caused a deep sleep to fall on Adam, and he slept; and He took one of his ribs, and closed up the flesh in its place.

Then the rib which the LORD God had taken from man He made into a woman, and He brought her to the man.

—GENESIS 2:18, 21, 22

As you read this book, you will see what a marriage should not be. One that just endures life, one that dishonors and constantly demeans the other, and dishonors God, certainly does not provide a good model for your children, friends, or in-laws.

Let's look at what a great marriage is and how one can last for eternity. I should be the one to talk, you are probably saying, since mine was mediocre at best and ended in divorce. I would have agreed with you a year ago, but now that I have gone through a long-endured relationship and recovered from divorce and resurrected my heart and soul, I am in a great position to give you what I think makes a great marriage and also one aligned with the biblical principles and a true loving heart.

Based on the divorce rate of over 50 percent, the deck is stacked against us and that is unacceptable to me and should be to you. Even Christians have done a poor job at marriage and need to start reversing those numbers.

As I grow older, I've noticed I have changed. I no longer do the things I did in my twenties and thirties, and maturity has taken hold somewhat. After years went by and friends started to marry, we shifted a little in our phase of life. The weekend parties and spur-of-the-moment meetings slowed, and then became nonexistent. Once children entered the marriage, things between spouses changed again. We put all our focus on the children and their activities, and lost ourselves. We lost our identities and questioned what we were in the marriage for, and became exhausted with children and work.

Life is like seasons, changing with each passing of the calendar months. In the career cycle, some change jobs and some lose them with the added stress of maintaining the household and trying to keep it together while unemployed. Some allow that stress to beat them up and start the cycle of guilt, shame, and other emotions the enemy loves to fill our heads with, and this can lead to a destructive marriage. It's the enemy's goal for all marriages to fail so he gets the upper hand and can bring discontinuity to God's children and decrease the numbers. It's our job to recognize this and be prepared for the enemy's hits: rest assured that with God's help and our whole heart we will prevail and the enemy will lose. Stay in the faith and love with your true heart and you will win.

What is common in most divorces is that the couple married young and just endured the passing of time until they no longer had it in them to continue the relationship. Being weighed down with life's adversities we choose not to handle correctly, we let the enemy get the upper hand and destroy our marriages. We never changed with the times and adapted to the situation, and as we got older we started to accuse the other that it was their fault we were unhappy. Then we sought counseling or tried to buy our way out with material items and nothing seemed to work. We thought distractions like a new car or home improvement or a vacation were the fix. Neither of us was willing to take ownership of the relationship problem. When we married no one talked about the success of marriage in terms of eternity with his or her new spouse; instead the talk was always about the easy way out using divorce.

Now in my forties, I have a different, much more mature, view of life. I have for the first time seen that the young adults out of college and looking to make a name in corporate America are desperate for their own identities. Then throw in marriage when you don't know the whos, whats, wheres, whens, whys, and hows of yourself. If we just take the time to figure out who we are and what God has planned for us, and mature with that for several years, then we can consider getting married and starting a family. The cost and stress associated with marriage and raising a family is the leading cause of all divorce. You graduate from college with student loans and maybe a car payment and credit card debit. Now you marry and combine debt, not assets. This is the beginning of an induced stress the enemy loves. He will lure you with debt, sex, fun, and the image of a family, with a white picket fence, and you need to start now, not later. So we rush into marriage based on feelings of love or because it feels like the right thing to do at the time, but whatever the case take a look at yourself and when you got married and the scenario, and most likely you will go, *Wow.*

We should wait for a while before getting married and look at what marriage really is, not a lifelong commitment to misery. Couples should be counseled before the marriage ceremony; it needs to be taken seriously and with the right person and not a stand-in. So how can we do this and make it work? I am not sure, but I will give you my changed vision of what marriage is and should be, now that I am older, wiser, and have lived through many mistakes.

Marriage is a relationship that God has brought together as man and woman as written in Genesis. It starts with the key ingredient, love from a true whole heart. What is love? The Bible tells us in Corinthians:

> *Love is patient, love is kind. It does not envy, it does not boast, it is not proud. It does not dishonor others, it is not self-seeking, it is not easily angered, it keeps no records of wrongs. Love does not delight in evil but rejoices with the truth. It always protects, always trusts, always hopes, always perseveres.*
>
> —1 CORINTHIANS 13:4–7

> *And now these three remain: faith, hope, and love. But the greatest of these is love.*
>
> —1 CORINTHIANS 13:13

Marriage is naturally enjoyed by both and not forced on another. It is a relationship that has the core values of love, trust, respect, and integrity. It is a relationship that can uphold 1 Corinthians 13 and its principles. It's a relationship that makes a man become selfless to his wife. In marriage a man and woman become one flesh and live as though they are one. It is a relationship that actively communicates and one that has you engaged when your spouse speaks to you and vice versa. Marriage has you daily, weekly, and monthly studying her wants and needs. Look at her expression when she talks: Is she smiling, distressed, or just communicating and wants you to listen? Look, listen, and learn, and your spouse will do the same for you. Pay her compliments and encourage her, become an inspiration to her and one she looks up to. Women want to be heard and men need to get better at listening to them. We each have our own uniqueness and that's what makes it tough when we cohabit. Learn to compromise when needed and discuss, not argue, about a plan or point. To start out right in marriage will allow you to successfully see forty years together of pure enjoyment. It takes work for a relationship to stand the test of time. Be positive and always encourage each other, and that day will come.

Be the spiritual leader of your household and watch what God does to your relationship. If this is your second or even third chance, as mine will be someday, make this the best of you anyone has ever seen. Enjoy life and the new you that gives love unconditionally to the lucky woman God will put into your life. This relationship should reflect a natural, unscripted happiness to those around you. Your life together should always look forward in a positive manner to where you see yourselves in eternity. The relationship requires maintenance as other things in life do, like your body, your car, and your house, and to prevent parts from breaking down, they need a routine tune-up. Do this by paying attention to yourselves and don't forget when life becomes busy with career and raising children. Plan on every other year getting away with your spouse and tune up your marriage. Go out for dinners a couple of times a month with just you two and no distractions. When you first met you always did things that involved being together, so don't lose that. Remember what it was and revisit how you were before the busy days of your life. It is truly amazing what a few nights a week together, whether at home or out, will do for you. Just pay attention to your spouse and never give up on them, as they will be there when you need them the most.

So you're probably still saying, okay, so why didn't you do these things, Brian? The answer is because I was with the wrong person from the start and the true love I speak of here was not there, and the personality of my ex-wife was one that did not work well with me.

I tried to make it right and learned that you cannot force love; it is just there and very much earned like respect and not given. Love comes from your true heart of hearts and when your heart is whole and true, and you will know when you find love. You will question its validity and maybe even try to push it away. You may feel like you never felt before, but can recognize with your maturity what you're confronted with. Today's culture is tough on marriages as we have become a materialistic society and watch reality TV showing bad marriages. This puts pressure on couples to earn money for buying certain items that only bring temporary happiness. So the husband and wife work a lot and focus on what's important to them individually, not the relationship. It's a juggling act to find the sweet spot in life. If you have little debt and no reason to put extra pressure on the relationship from the bondage debt creates, then you have lessened the noose that money has on your marriage.

Marriage with pure, unrestricted love is the best on the planet. It is a love that shines with God's smile daily. Living with the daily feeling of joy and positive spirit from the one in your life is courtesy of God Almighty, and the best gift He has given to us.

I know this sounds like fairy-tale lies, but I tell you it is not. Marriage, love, family, and careers are a tough juggling act, but well rewarded when you are with the spouse God intended you to have and you find the sweet spot in the hierarchy of what is important to your relationship.

Initially when my son Brian asked me for my thoughts on marriage I thought about how marriage has changed over the last five decades and more since I was a child.

Back in the fifties marriage in America was mostly between a man and woman of the same race and religion, united for the purpose of having children. Mom usually stayed home and Dad was the proud provider. The family worshiped together in a local church.

Fast-forward, and marriage today in our country has changed in many ways. It is now the union of two people and not necessarily for the purpose of having children. The couple may be of completely different backgrounds, races, and religions. Quite often both people are working and sharing in household duties or the raising of children. Percentage wise, not as many families attend church on a regular basis.

The basic fundamentals of a successful marriage are pretty much the same though: trust, sharing, respect, caring for one another in good times as well as bad, showing appreciation for one another, commitment, communication, and honesty. Most of all there should be a strong friendship, everlasting love, and a shared belief in a higher power.

—Janet Nastovski

The forty-eight hours after my initial shock were filled with denial and deep sadness. I felt failure and guilt, and questioned what was happening. Sadly, I had told myself for years I wanted out of my marriage. Now I felt betrayed, asking myself, "How dare she tell me to get out of the life we built together?"

I wasn't ready to walk away but my heart felt tender and stomped, my manhood wiped away. I felt like a huge failure to Kate, my children, and myself. Daddy was about to leave them behind. Kate probably felt abandoned, broken, and resentful. She had stopped working to be home with our children and might have felt inadequate to provide for her and the children without my full financial support.

It appeared Kate experienced depression and many of the same feelings I was working through. Low self-esteem, doubt, and insecurity seemed to be rampaging for both of us. I had never seen Kate battling these emotional depths. She was a hardworking mom and had accomplished much in the volunteer world. As den leader for our sons' Cub

Scout pack, she helped raise young boys into young men by leading the once-a-week meetings. She continued with the Troop in Boy Scouts and served as a committee member. She was a gifted planner and organizer for meetings and events like campouts. These events had an incredible impact on our sons growing up.

Feelings of desperation cause fear about the future, making your brain question how will you be able to maintain the lifestyle you have enjoyed together. Neither she nor I would have the same lifestyle. Sacrifices were made for our children to have their needs met and hopefully some of their wants. As her fear grew, it appeared she focused on me as her enemy. Our relationship grew tenser and I felt hurt and angry. Allowing God to fill my heart each morning kept me from making matters worse. Without Him, this story would read differently. If you see yourself in this scenario, know it will pass. Hang on, do your best to respond with gentleness, and do not get into shouting matches. The arguments are a waste of time and energy, causing an increase in your blood pressure and weighing you down with anger toward the mother of your children. Ultimately, this just crushes your day. Fighting fire with fire doesn't work.

This is where the focus on God is so important. God has a better plan on how to handle these issues, so just keep asking Him. Read His word and you will hear Him speaking to your heart, instructing you along the way.

I was not an angel as we walked through the division of our lives. Just to be clear, I am not pointing out my ex-wife Kate as bad. I simply feel it is important to relay how we failed in order to help you avoid pitfalls, if possible. Emotions are part of our being and they work overtime, even when we are praying to stay calm or stand strong. All negative emotions result from dwelling on negative thoughts and allowing them power over our actions.

> *And the peace of God, which transcends all understanding, will guard your hearts and your minds in Christ Jesus.*
>
> *Finally, brothers and sisters, whatever is true, whatever is noble, whatever is right, whatever is pure, whatever is lovely, whatever is admirable—if anything is excellent or praise-worthy—think about such things.*
>
> *Whatever you have learned or received or heard from me, or seen in me—put it into practice. And the God of peace will be with you.*
>
> —PHILIPPIANS 4:7–9

We have all experienced situations where a discussion dissolves into a disagreement, and often one person in the conversation becomes angry and starts shouting. When you argue with them, the point of discussion is changed to a personal attack. All parties involved are soon exhausted from the energy expended on hurting each other. Another example is when the man who dislikes his current job, position, or workplace focuses on the environment's faults, and convinces himself the place created his state of mind. I contend we have complete control over our emotional responses, even to bad situations. Instead concentrate on your inner strength promised and provided by the Holy Spirit and change your attitude. Most often your environment will change too. At least your outlook will change and allow you to walk into situations with a powerful stance of joy. Allow hurtful words to hit and brush them off like dust or dandruff. Remember the saying "Sticks and stones may break my bones, but words will never hurt me." Words *can* hurt if we allow them to penetrate our belief system. When we are confident in God's word and love for us, few words break through our shield of faith (again, provided by God's Holy Spirit living within us).

Many of us were not taught how to communicate our emotions or identify them. Although we started early, learning basic principles of emotions, we lost the momentum as we approached adulthood. It's important to revisit the lesson combined with God's grace to guard your heart. Practiced often, this will become one of the best character building exercises you've experienced.

I lost who I was and allowed myself to become a victim based on *guilt*. Rather than serving God and following His plan, I served my own hidden guilt feelings. God was prompting me to confess and repent— His path to freedom.

> *Then I acknowledge my sin to you and did not cover up my iniq-uity. I said, "I will confess my transgressions to the LORD." And you forgave the guilt of my sin.*
> —PSALM 32:5

The vicious cycle in arguing and demeaning her as she hurt me was unproductive in our relationship and of course not the way God wanted us to deal with it. I became someone I did not know and turned to the "he said, she said" circle of defending my reasoning as to why we said what we did to the other.

We tried counseling years ago, but for whatever reason it didn't work and I blew it off and she continued for a few more sessions without me. We were so busy defending our different points, which was so wrong and did nothing but make us feel so hurt and drained. I remember the counselor, who was Christian-based, say, "You guys do one thing great together, and that's argue."

So I asked myself the who, what, where, when, why, and how of our relationship to analyze where I went wrong and how I allowed this to happen. Could I have prevented this? Why did I not see the signs and say, stop, mayday, critical failure is about to take place. I did see the signs years ago so the question became why did we continue to endure a bad relationship versus enjoy it? I am not sure, but I think we were staying together for the children plus the daily busyness of life with jobs and family allowed us to deny the obvious and then we did things like try to buy the love we didn't have and soon found out that didn't work either. I lost focus on God and myself and that was when the tailspin began. I had checked out of my marriage years ago and never checked back in. I remember when I drove home from work I felt a change come about, and became depressed as I changed into that other person, the one who did not want to be there and knew what I would experience when I walked through the door. I will not speak for my ex-wife, only myself, and she tried to make us work, she really did. She had books for me to read and I never read them. She always had some suggestion I never took.

I look back and say I wasn't ready. It wasn't until the divorce that I became the man she was looking for. I do not have any answers to why

I did not take her suggestions, other than to say I had checked out big time and the enemy was winning for sure.

Once we check out, it's extremely hard to return as the enemy has you in his grip and will do everything to keep you, and it takes amazing will, strength, and faith to pull out of the catatonic state you are in. For me, the divorce was an event that led me to change myself. I told her I was sorry for not reading those books, but I am reading now and taking charge of my life, and changing myself to become the man God wants me to be. This man has a whole heart, an awesome caring soul, is a loving father to his children, and serves others and brings the greatness out of them the way God wants. That was when the rewards started to happen. I lived a Christ-like life the best I could and exercised the things I was learning daily. The road to recovery got easier with each passing day and I let nothing and no one destroy the joy of my day, and I did not let those crazy emotions get the best of me. I concentrated on my children like never before and started talking to them individually as I took each to dinner at a place of their choice.

One evening the waitress came over and asked what was the special occasion with my son. I said every day is special with my son. We are here just to eat and talk. She couldn't believe it and was so happy to see that. After I spent the time to get me right, I started getting right with my children and the feedback coming in was positive. I can't thank God enough for the healing he has brought me so quickly and through me to my children.

Chapter 9

The Scales of Justice

K ate's attorney was the most negative person I have ever dealt with, and known in attorney circles as the Bulldog of Orlando. I'm not sure how many divorce attorneys are positive in nature as they are always in an emotional battle with their clients, plus the daily fighting with other attorneys. It has to be the worst job, seeing day in and day out the emotional trauma the client goes through, and parents dragging children into their mess as pawns in this crazy game of threats and broken promises. If you see any chance of reconciliation, a divorce attorney can ruin that by asking for everything you own and wedging you and your wife apart further due to the feelings of hatred bolstered by them. They play on that hatred and do their best to stop any progress.

After my dealings with the attorney, I decided to not let her get the best of me and destroy at least a friendship with my wife. I felt like I was divorcing her attorney too.

The attorney wanted everything plus lifetime alimony based on our years of marriage. I was not expecting such a proposal supported by

Kate. I had yet to secure an attorney, and Kate explained that all I had to do was read the proposal, sign it, and we could have the divorce finalized in thirty days using her attorney.

After I heard this, I knew it was time for an attorney. I hired one and we pored over the document.

The first thing that was apparent was her attorney's appearance of greed. The initial draft had nothing in it for me other than my bike, television, and 401(k). She took everything else plus child support and lifetime alimony. I was appalled at the demands being made and let my emotions get the best of me, which was wrong.

My attorney said, "Brian, you need to calm down and let us do our job." This was my life and not his. As I drove back home, I thought, *He's right. He doesn't tell me how to do my job, so why should I tell him how to do his?* He did say that he never spoke to a divorce attorney so angry in spirit over the phone and that made me get worried again. After leaving my attorney's office, I called Kate to tell her I had reviewed the proposal. She asked if I had signed it and I said no. She expected me to sign over my entire life to her as a token of appreciation for her divorcing me. From what I could tell from our conversation, she said the divorce would cost *x* amount of money with two attorneys. I said it would save me much more in the end and I had to protect myself. She allowed fear and the attorney doing her job to translate the divorce into monetary gains and personal revenge.

Within a week Kate and I had a conversation and she asked me why I was going out to eat and spending money on my personal credit card, as she had learned from the statements she viewed online. She was a joint cardholder, with me as primary holder. I controlled the emotion being displayed to me and ended her as a secondary cardholder, and changed the password on the account so that she could not view it anymore. It was very clear that she could not accept that I was going out to eat while she was home with the children. The question is why she looked or even cared. She still wanted to see what I was doing with my life and where was I going.

When your mind is so numb that you become jealous of your ex-husband's going out to eat, it's time to start the true separation to prevent such emotion from getting in the way. I was the one who had left everything behind and needed to eat to survive, who lived in an apartment with no cookware or furniture.

I paid all the bills for our house yet never questioned how she spent the money I gave her. Now that she could no longer read the credit card statements, it wouldn't get to her. I know there are many emotions that come to the surface during a divorce, and some never felt before, but I couldn't understand why she allowed herself to let them control her. I was showing her I could live on my own and I didn't need her to tell me when the card had to be paid or when my rent was due. Between that and giving her money the same day I was paid, I tried to build her trust in me that I would take care of her financially.

Kate called her attorney and the attorney sent my attorney a scathing letter of how I was going to financially ruin her and harm the children due to not giving them enough money. They were always taken care of and still are, and I have never let her down when it came to keeping her financially secure.

It's another tactic divorce attorneys use so that you fall on your knees early and sign the agreement and your life away due to your emotionally distraught state, but I didn't go for it.

The days of control were over and I prepared for the battle of my life. Kate's attorney advised her to take half of the savings right now, as if I was going to leave her and the children without a penny. I never touched the bank account until several months after my wife took her portion, and her withdrawal proved to be another example of mistrust by her and her attorney.

The hardest thing I had to do was get my emotions under control. I saw the woman who had never displayed this type of greed toward me suddenly doing this and very angrily. I continued to pray for emotional relief and that I would not let those worries weigh me down.

I allowed them to get in my head and was unable to control my thoughts. I finally had to snap out of it and fought to control my emotions about the divorce. I was not ready at all. I challenged her every demand while constantly paying all the bills for her and for myself as I reestablished my life. It seemed that every request from her was for money. She wanted half of my paycheck and yet I wasn't being fair by giving her only that much. Next I heard that since I was able to work overtime on my days off to make more for myself, she got less so that was also not fair. How the mind gets into that mess. She never once considered a job or that I would be giving her x amount of dollars with alimony and child support; then she did find a job later and supplemented the money I gave her, the same as me working overtime she had complained about.

You see where her mind went out of control and became a financial *want machine*.

Once she said, "I want it all," like Veruca Salt in *Willy Wonka and the Chocolate Factory*, in the scene where Veruca wants the goose that lays golden eggs and her daddy asks Wonka how much. My wife's fear of the unknown made it appear that greed was the motive. Greed never prevails and all involved with it end up finishing last instead of winning.

> *For the love of money is a root of all kinds of evil, for which some have strayed from faith in their greediness, and pierced them-selves through with many sorrows.*
>
> —1 TIMOTHY 6:10

Kate wanted her life to be the same it had been throughout our marriage, just minus me. The attorney she had firmly supported her behavior and invigorated it most likely by saying, *You will get it all*. At times I felt she was the best actress on the planet. My advice to men going through divorce is be careful and listen to your gut and lawyer, and don't get emotionally caught up to where you are drained and give everything to her and leave yourself penniless on a lifetime alimony payment, having to rebuild your life.

Her attorney used language toward me that set me off every time I received a letter from her and I had to figure out how to remain calm. When I received a letter advising me of two motions filed against me, one for the total bill if we went to court that I would be responsible for, and the other a huge monthly payment in support above what I was already giving her, I almost lost it again.

This is how her attorney made money off my situation and I did not like this at all. I kept seeing my children having their finances stripped from them with these unnecessary motions that could have been prevented.

The first motion was for attorney fees, since Kate wasn't working, with a proposed amount if we took our case to court for litigation. We were not solving our problems and she was going to leave me broke. The monthly support payment motion was dropped but the other court costs stayed.

Now I had to pay the fees for filing of the motion by my attorney and hers, and then the cost to see it in court. My attorney fought this in court and they dismissed the order for full coverage of a court battle, but ordered me to pay up to a maximum in attorney fees for Kate and do so in a ninety-day period. Why was I the one paying the bill and she had zero responsibility? After six months there were still no wins for me in the divorce, only the bill. I felt as if my children were the ones losing out as my wife filed frivolous motions. I was very upset with the way her mind was working, and I believed she was out for herself and not the children based on the information I had at the time and I didn't like what she was becoming. After nineteen years together, I thought we could come to a reasonable solution, but not when divorce attorneys were involved.

Kate's attorney was still adamant that I pay all fees in this divorce, even after the judge said only up to what he ordered, with my wife to pay the remainder on her own.

Through this I stayed the calm, although I did not attend the hearing for the motions because of work. Her attorney was not pleased with my absence. I would get my day to see her face-to-face in mediation, and stand tall like Maximus in the film *Gladiator*, and greed would not prevail on that day.

I would not let her attorney get to me or be drawn into her world during her opening remarks. I would remain calm, expressionless, and strong. I would show up ready for battle and do so in a professional manner, and show her I was the one man she could not defeat. I prepared by embracing my emotional, spiritual, and physical side. This made me stronger than ever and I would put all three into play for this very trying time.

There is no user manual, no quick reference handbook or checklist regarding divorce and when to do things and how to do them. The trauma of divorce is as bad as you let it, so this was my time to be strong and begin my new journey. I decided to attack the problem as if I had cancer and was going to beat it. Battling and never giving up on myself as if today was my last day worked great and allowed me to focus on what was important, and allowed me to get physically much stronger.

In a situation like divorce you need take time off from work and regroup, and simply breathe. Then start preparing your new life plan. Get a lawyer and prepare yourself for a journey of six months to one year, unless you can come to an agreement with your spouse and carry out a do-it-yourself divorce, but you still have to wait a long time with the court system.

List all your assets and liabilities on paper when your head clears. Once you establish a residence and start rebuilding your life with new furnishings, keep any receipts: you will need them to prove your current living expenses to the attorneys.

Get yourself mentally and financially stable before worrying about your children. If you're no good, your children will not be good either, so take care of yourself now and build your support group. Some of your friends will not want to be bothered with your discussion of divorce, yet others, your real friends, will always listen. Many churches have great divorce-recovery programs and I recommend looking into one; they will make a great support group for you. My dad always said, "In divorce your spouse can take your money, your house, and your kids, but she or he cannot take your mind." Anything can be replaced except for your mind. Lose your mind you lose yourself. Stay strong, stay healthy, and don't allow yourself to be obsessive and overanalyze. This creates worry.

You will know when you're doing it right; what you're doing for yourself is hard. It takes a lot of effort to look at one's heart and soul and fight for your marriage and not want divorce if possible. Next you must take care of the bills and go to work as if nothing has happened and get back into daily life so your mind can get off the subject during the day. The easier route from separation to divorce is not doing anything but lying around not paying bills. Getting right into another relationship fresh from your separation has an 85 percent chance of not surviving. You may even start hanging out with the wrong crowd and if you don't take care of yourself, your health diminishes and mental acuity starts to lessen when you need clarity. It's important to take the time you are given during a separation and start rebuilding the rest of your life. Change your heart and it will change you.

Chapter 10

Moving Day

After living at my dad's for a while, I leased a one-bedroom apartment. Here is where I threw caution to the wind regarding apartment living. If I could have afforded a house, I would have. It all started the afternoon I went to the local gym to cancel our joint membership and my wife's personal trainer. I then said, "Brian, it's time to be by yourself." I love my dad and stepmom, but I was forty-three years old and had to figure this out on my own. So I called a rental agency and they said they had an apartment ready for immediate occupancy. I met with the salesman and had the weird feeling of, *What in the heck am I doing here?*

He asked me why I was looking for an apartment. I was not prepared for that question and I answered I was going through a divorce. We went to look at the apartment and I felt euphoric, like I wasn't there but I was. After looking at the property, all I remember is the gym. We went back to the office and I signed a lease that would allow me out with only a minimal charge and no security deposit. At five o'clock that afternoon, I received the keys and moved my stuff in the following day. I slept on an air mattress for three months and had no furniture. I wasn't ready to admit I had failed as a husband and a man. I was all screwed up. I hadn't lived in an apartment in over twenty two years and what an experience it was. I used each day for reflection into my past and talked to God a lot; without distractions I was able to quickly figure me out. The other tenants were local college kids, partying all the time and loud music some nights.

The wall in my bedroom was next to a staircase, thank you Mr. Architect, and it was noisy most nights with the climbing and the kids hanging out talking.

My next-door neighbor had two little dogs and when he left they barked for hours, so I banged on the wall until they quieted down. The neighbor across the hall played music so loudly it screamed through his walls. My neighbor directly overhead had a three-year-old child I called the Energizer Bunny. The kid ran back and forth over my head daily, until midnight some nights, and I spoke to the office five times about the problem and still the beat went on. That experience alone was like Chinese torture: kids running loose and the occasional wakeup from couples having sex above my head. Did I mention the fires and armed security patrol in my gated complex? A couple of months after I moved in, the neighbors upstairs and across the hall caught their apartment on fire. I came home to fire trucks and a flooded foyer. Later in March someone set the clubhouse bathroom on fire.

I needed to get out of there, but every time I said, "Easy, Brian, just breathe." Most mornings I sat on the bench and looked at the water, and just thought. It was a time I talked with my sister too. All the women in the complex owned dogs and walked them every morning and evening and there was dog poop everywhere. I wasn't ready to see women and wanted no part of them, and I wanted out of the situation I was in. It was almost Christmas, and that was when I decided to get my butt off the floor and buy furniture for the children and myself so that we'd feel secure and comfortable. My back was killing me as well.

When the children came to visit and saw the new furniture, their eyes lit up. The chairs had built-in recliners and the children were so excited, they each claimed one as their own. My daughter, Hannah, suffered from anxiety mostly due to the relationship she had endured with her mother and me, and for that I am so sorry, sweetheart. The boys were equally affected in ways that changed them for the worse. I saw the healing right before my eyes as Hannah's nausea from her anxiety disappeared and Chris's and Jason's spirits came back to life. The kids were in the man cave now—safe, comfortable, and full of love.

I bought a new camera to document my new life and take pictures of my kids. Life had changed when I looked through the viewfinder. I also bought a bed and the needed household items for daily living. Life was starting to reshape itself. The children have done so well and I am grateful for this. Although my being strong helps them, they are no longer in a bad situation with their mother and I know that was the biggest blessing they could have received. I will not forget the day soon after I had left when my oldest asked me, "Dad, how are we going to get money to eat and pay for the house with Mom?" My answer was simple: "You never have to worry as I will take care of you guys. You will always have a roof over your heads and food on the table." I have never let them down, or my ex-wife. They loved being with me and were happier than ever and that's all that mattered. After four months in the apartment, I decided it was time to look for a home.

I looked into high-rise apartment living and liked what I saw. The big problem for me was getting into the downtown party scene and possibly lose what I had worked so hard for. I thought maybe if I lived there I would meet a beautiful working professional woman making great money. The woman showing the apartment was beautiful and I thought maybe she was the type of woman who lived downtown. I started to feel distracted and did not like that, so I went back to the apartment to think. I asked myself, is this the right thing to do for me, or the kids? I said, no, it's all about the kids now. So I looked for a house instead because I wanted them to have that home feeling versus the downtown vibe, and home feeling was what they were used to. I started my search and found a two story home half a mile from the their high school. It had a pool on two lakes and a bedroom for each child. Now we could be as normal as normal can be in divorce. I learned it's about the children and not me at this point of my life, but I came first because if I wasn't happy, they wouldn't be, either.

I pursued the home rental scene and started my road to happiness that in turn made them happier.

God had picked the perfect setting for me to start my new journey with my three beautiful children. The home was very quiet compared to apartment life, but strangely too quiet without the noise of the children. I have rooster noise and turkeys in the early mornings, and such beautiful sunrises. I see the stars at night and the privacy behind as if I was out in the country. The children fell in love with the house right away and that's how I knew the decision was right. They checked the place out as if they were dogs, running around and smelling every corner. They took a mattress and slid down the stairs and I watched with a smile like never before. I have since stopped that for many reasons. They love fishing, so many of their days here are filled with fishing. We also go in the evening and find rabbits when they come out to feed. With the summer swimming and barbequing, it has been a dream come true for them.

Growing Up

> Every man was once a boy. And every little boy has dreams, big dreams: dreams of being the hero, of beating the bad guys, of doing daring feats and rescuing the damsel in distress.
>
> Every little girl has dreams, too: of being rescued by her prince and swept up into a great adventure, knowing that she is beauty.
>
> —FROM *WILD AT HEART* BY JOHN ELDREDGE

When you read the above, could you relate? Do you remember playing superheroes and wanting to be Superman and wearing a cape made of a beach towel? Do you remember saving the damsel in distress? I sure do. I pretended I was Evel Knievel for one day, and then Superman the next. I jumped off my garage roof, porch, or tree, whatever I could find to invoke adventure.

From the beginning men were meant to be warriors as God is. We were designed to fight and always look for adventure. When you watch movies like *Gladiator, Braveheart,* or *Saving Private Ryan,* do you feel the connection of the warrior spirit and the fight for what is right? The next time you watch these movies, watch them as if they are your story and feel the difference.

My sons, Chris and Jason, have fought each other with plastic light-sabers from *Star Wars* for years, and now they use the Styrofoam noodles in the pool. They tie a knot at one end and battle; I watch with great interest as the two boys whack each other and make red marks on their bodies. The oldest, Chris, always gets the best of his younger brother, but the warrior in Jason comes out and he never gives up; he keeps charging onward. They look to me and at some point I get involved as Goliath. We wrestle in the pool and my little girl, Hannah, joins in the drowning of Dad. Jason summed it up in a picture he drew for me. It was a picture of my bike and he wrote: *When you get a flat you keep going. One of our favorite things about you.*

When you get a flat you keep going. one of our favorit things a bout you.

The warrior in me has been shown to him through my actions; what wisdom from an eleven-year-old boy.

He has seen my physical change, from heavy to lean. He has seen me leave and make a new, happy life and also keep my children safe and secure, while never talking bad about their mother, only good, and only continuing to let them know how important God is in all our lives.

Chapter 11

Changing of the Heart

Keep your heart with all diligence, for out of it springs the issues of life.

—Proverbs 4:23

I began my journey to a changed heart very soon after leaving the home I had built with Kate. I had only an air mattress in the apartment, along with the back pillow I propped against the wall as I watched a little TV or read my books.

I wanted no distractions and dove right into my heart. It started with a message from Dr. James McDonald about forgiveness: *Look on my affliction and my pain, and forgive all my sins* (Psalm 25:18). This is when the change began in me. I felt the heavy burden of negativity disappear and be replaced with positive thoughts. I forgave my wife immediately and did so each day. Jesus said to forgive seven times seventy. I started to read the books of John Eldredge, recommended by a pastor at church. I saw life and good from bad, and I heard positive not negative thoughts. This was huge. My counselor kept me positive and I will never be able to thank him enough for the godly support he gave to me when I needed it the most.

> *Counsel in the heart of man is like deep water, but a man of understanding will draw it out.*
>
> —PROVERBS 20:5

I started counseling with a young man in training at a place in Orlando. I left after a few sessions because it wasn't doing what I wanted; the wisdom was far from what I needed but also he was new and we have to start somewhere. I needed more. He started the first session with, "Tell me three good things about your wife." I just cried.

I was hurting and he said, "Brian, you are really sad. I feel for you." It was time to seek higher ground and I thank you, God, for Pastor Kevin. I was paired up with Pastor Kevin and continued to visit him. Kevin is the kindest, most soft-spoken man I have met. When I started seeing him I asked myself why I was even there, and the answer was because I cared. I went with hopes of healing my pain so I could see clearly and maybe get my marriage back.

I discovered instead I was battling for myself, as we can only fix ourselves with God, no one else. I was in a battle for the heart and soul I had allowed to be taken away over the years. What was God up to and what was his plan? As I journeyed through the life-changing experience, I asked God many times, "Why me, and what do You want me to do with the information I have learned?" I put it to use in regaining my heart and soul. And so a story was born, the story you are reading.

We all have a story to tell, but most never do. I felt that God was calling me to share my story with men all over the world in the hope that I could bring motivation and inspiration so that they will heal their hearts and win back their souls. I started classes at Northland to fulfill a promise to myself and God, in His honor. I didn't know the first thing about writing so just kept a daily record of my thoughts for months. Then I began to figure out my writing style based on the books I was reading. Writing this book has been the best experience in my life and brought such healing and comfort.

I leaned on God for his words in prayer and He spoke through me to you.

As you continue to read, think about the value of counseling in pastoral form and the biblical form of God's word.

I read the Bible again, as that was my true counselor, and really heard from God. I started to get it clear again and it was good to be back. I took my new energy to fight for my wife again. I went back to her with my newly healed heart, and she wanted nothing to do with me. That hurt.

Kate was amazed at the change in me, so much that it seemed untrue to her, coming so quickly. Maybe it was an act. She said, "Why didn't you change before this happened?" and why this and why that. She was mad because I was doing what she had wanted me to do for years. Better late than never, I thought, and God had the plan and timing. He had picked that moment to change me and I accepted.

I lived on my own, paid my own bills, and started the journey to become the best father I have ever known, and started to pay attention to my appearance. For Kate's birthday, I decided to make homemade cannoli from my mother's Old World Italian recipe. This was after only two weeks of being out of the house. I did not have any pans or cookware, so I used a friend's equipment and their kitchen to make the filling. This was the first time I had made the filling. I then bought the shells and filled them at my apartment. All the while I was spinning from what was going on and wanting my wife back so badly. The trauma was still so fresh and the fight in me got stronger for both of us, but mostly me. She gave me no real response other than thanks, just pure ice. Her sternness blanked me out and she would not give in to my kindness and allow me back into her life. This was her way of guarding what could be an act on my part to get back into the marriage, and once again have the past repeat itself. She wanted no part of that.

It was my first attempt to fight for her beauty, and she was slipping away very quickly. Unless you have another woman in your life through an affair, I believe we instinctively fight, even if for the wrong reasons, for the current woman in your life. It's just how we were made to be true warriors. This was a fight for her heart, a battle for her beauty, and a bunch of setbacks in the process for me. I now know it was an exercise in building my character and spirit, and God saw me through this when I laid all my trust in His hands.

Chapter 12

The Cycle Clears My Head and Where I Talk with God

got on my bike and pedaled for miles to relive myself of the emotional unbalance I felt as I struggled with the question of why do I still want to be with her after what she says to me and I say to her. More important: Do I have what it takes to get through this divorce?

My first century ride, which consists of one hundred miles of cycling, was on Halloween 2010 and also my first holiday apart from the children. The ride was really great until the last fifteen miles; I had cramps in my right calf but powered through. It was a crazy ride from the beginning. We took off at a twenty-three- to twenty-four-mph pace in our peloton bunch for the first thirty miles. I got to the eighty-mile point and told the group to go ahead as I wanted to enjoy the last twenty miles. At times I was all by myself and talked to my wife in my head about basic stuff, as if I had never known her. Was I getting dehydrated and delirious? I met up with the ride organizer and he gave me an awesome tour in the last ten miles. I stopped for a burger at a fast-food place and could not eat, like my stomach had shrunk. I burned close to five thousand calories on that ride and my body was messed up from power gels and Gatorade.

When I returned from my ride, I didn't have much time to rest because I wanted to go trick-or-treating with my children that evening. My legs hurt and I was hungry but I wanted to be with them so much that I kept going without letting on to my exhaustion. I wanted to put my feet up and start the recovery process and sleep. Instead I walked miles with my legs cramping a little every now and then, but there was no way I wouldn't be there with them. I sucked up the pain and enjoyed the moment with them and would never change it for a minute. The next holiday was Thanksgiving, and that was when I knew I would be apart from my family forever. I spent that holiday at the friend of a friend's after a fifty-mile bike ride. I couldn't help but think about my children and wife many times during dinner. I was settling to being divorced. Christmas was next and I decided it was time for me to start the rebuilding process and get on with life. I bought furniture, a bed, and cooking equipment. Next I bought plates and bowls, and real eating utensils instead of plastic forks and spoons. Because of the fluidity of my situation and duration of my sixteen-year marriage, I thought we would get back together at some point. My children and I deserved better than what I was currently providing us. We needed the feel of a home and the security in that environment. No more plastic forks and paper bowls and bare floors. It was time to let these children see their dad become the man God made him to be, and look out, here I come. I started to listen to my children and paid attention to each like never before. I was getting connected to them and, boy, it was great. On New Year's Eve and the beginning of 2011, I sent a text to my wife and said Happy New Year. She did not reply, as was the case with most of the texts I had sent her lately with positive comments.

My heart started to heal, and I accepted the fact that most likely I would end up divorced and there was no hope for fixing the mess. I knew when I left there would be no return for me; once I am gone, I am gone. I became an optimistic realist. I was optimistic that I could work hard at the relationship if given the chance, but also realistic that we would be divorced.

I decided that for the sake of the children, and myself too, it was time to forget about winning back my wife. I had to make their life as happy as could be in our situation; that was a challenge I greatly accepted. In February I decided I had to leave my small one-bedroom apartment, to give them a life that promoted happiness and healing for all of us. The lakes behind the home are awesome for bass fishing and Jason and Hannah do lots of it. They feel like it is Christmas each time they are here. My investment in them has paid huge dividends in their happiness, and mine.

Chapter 13

Boot Camp for the Heart and Soul

A t the end of March 2011, it was time for the Wild at Heart Boot Camp with John Eldredge. I had never been so nervous in wanting to get there and meet the band of brothers and start tying up the loose ends in my journey toward a new heart and soul and become a real man. I flew into Denver the night before to get some sleep and be ready for the next morning without having to worry about the flight being on time in the morning of the first day. I took the hotel shuttle to the airport and met where we were told. There were four or five buses waiting and the crowd started to build. Four hundred and fifty men were looking for the same things: a heart and soul and what bus they were supposed to get on. Some were pretty messed up but we were all brothers and it was amazing to see how many men wanted to make a change for the better. I applaud every one of them for coming out and sharing their stories. When mealtime came the men talked about their problems in a very constructive way with no real venting. I heard everything from divorce to alcoholism to sexual addiction. During downtime or around the fire pit with a manly cigar, the men continued their discussions about why they were there and what they expected to get out of the camp. It was my best experience as a man changing his heart.

The lesson was simple: care enough about yourself that you want to change you for you, and the fixing can only come from you and no one else. You can seek help but any counselor can only deliver the information you need, so it's up to you to use that information and fix yourself for yourself and no one else. After an experience like the boot camp, use the momentum to stay in the heart-changing game. Go home and allow yourself time to let the ideas soak in and begin a plan to help maintain the new heart. I purposely leave out the details of the camp so that you feel what I did in every form. You have to keep reading and talking about the changing of your heart, maybe enroll in classes at your church or volunteer to teach classes at your church.

Stay positive; get rid of the negative thoughts and always refill the tank with positive thoughts. Never stop encouraging yourself, as it may be tough finding those around you to offer encouragement while going through this transformation. Tell yourself you have what it takes and you are a good person. Look in the mirror and say you look great, do whatever it takes to pat yourself on the back with encouragement. Never give up and never let anyone take your joy away. Learning to be positive is very hard; for some reason we all have an easier time focusing on the negative, whether it's about the company we work for or people we know. It is worth the effort to become positive and find positive-thinking friends, as your body will respond to the effect big time. When your body lives in a negative environment, it changes for the worse.

Stress will make your skin breakout, possibly thin your hair, and have an effect on your heart in a damaging way. Stress is a known killer, so get rid of it. Once you gather all the positive feelings you can, they become part of your daily life. Your body will thank you and repair itself.

I used to have bad cracked skin on my fingers due to stress but since my transformation it's no more. My skin is smooth and my hair is fuller again, with the help of some topical treatment too, but overall I have really changed during this rebuilding and recharging of the positive in my life.

Chapter 14

The Physical Side

started riding my road bike about ten months before the legal separation due to the stress and had lost close to seventy pounds during this transformation.

My brother was responsible for getting me on my bike and getting my life back and for my first great bike. For that, Steve, I will be forever grateful to you, brother. God has given us a great gift in each other, and the help we share when in need. As my separation progressed, I rode farther and faster, and got stronger.

By March 2011, I had already completed three one-hundred-mile cycling rides either in a sponsored event or charity ride, and rode approximately 5,500 miles in that one year alone.

Biking or whatever exercise you choose will keep your mind clean and body strong. Exercise is the best way to take away the stress on your mind and body, chase away depression, and fill you with life.

I used my divorce as the catalyst for a positive change in my life, not negative, so I embarked on what I called *ESP*, the emotional, spiritual and physical attributes of living well. The physical side allowed me to drop from a forty-two-inch waist to thirty-two inches, and from weighing 270 pounds with almost 40 percent body fat to 195 pounds, and lean and mean at 6 percent body fat. The cardiovascular aspect of riding allowed the fat to melt away once my metabolism kicked in. I rode like crazy to beat the stress and that was when I noticed the change in my body. So I decided to keep this life pattern forever. I feel the best I've ever felt and also it has given me a way to maintain my health. I also began to work out at the gym four to five days a week and started to rebuild my physique. I have come a long way for a forty-four-year-old man, and so can you. This is your time; use it to get your mind and body healthy.

If you're not already there, get your finances straight and refocus on a new set of priorities, then get your mind prepared for the biggest round of emotional games you've ever experienced.

You must have strength and courage to endure the battle, and positive friends during this time. This is where I usually break out into one of my *Braveheart* speeches to rally the troops but I won't this time.

The early lessons for me were: number one, stay out of the bars; number two, stay away from women until your divorce is final, unless you're in an affair now and then think about slowing that down so you can keep your attention on what is important and that's you. You will be so focused on you that nothing else matters—that's if you're doing this in a way that its complete focus is on you. Take this opportunity to get close to your brothers and sisters and listen to them as they can provide great feedback. The feedback from them will generally be honest and true and what you need. You may not like what you hear, but they have your best interests at heart. Take what you can use and leave the rest, just don't get upset with them. If you're not close, use this experience to allow that to happen and become close to your siblings again. My sister Michelle has been my most valuable player during this divorce in her role of the listener. My mom listened a lot too, and to both of them I will never be able to find the words to express my gratitude for what they have done during this life-changing event. Michelle never said she did not have time to listen and I thank her for that. She saw God's work right before her eyes, changing my heart and soul. Emotionally get it together and work on you, then return to God if you were away, and exercise and focus on your children.

Stay away from the bitterness of nasty language that divorce brings out because it does nothing but forfeit your joy. You can use this experience and exercise in character building to reshape yourself, make you better for everyone around you, and for that next relationship. That will come and you will be anew, with a heart filled with love, gentleness, joy, and forgiveness, and the woman receiving this new you will be forever grateful. Your heart will be one that is wise and good and allow change to happen, and allow you to speak with the deep conviction of your experience. God meant for us to be with women, so enjoy the new relationship when it happens and treat your new girlfriend with more respect than has ever been given before.

The next thing you will receive is a new set of eyes. You will clearly see the true woman you were married to, and the old you and life in a new colorful way that resembles the first day of spring when the flowers awaken and bloom.

Think of what makes you and your heart come alive. This is a great scripture to memorize and use in the beginning of healing your heart:

> *And you will seek Me and find Me, when you search for Me with all your heart.*
>
> —JEREMIAH 29:13

The Hunt Calms My Spirit

I started deer hunting and bow hunting in 2007 with a friend who lived in New York and also with my father-in-law at his hunting camp. After buying a bow set, I went to a local sports center and learned to shoot. Shooting my first feral hog was a great feeling. The hunting experience brings me pure calmness and also a great sense of adventure. I love the morning hunt, an afternoon nap, and back out to hunt again. The evenings are set with bonfires, cigars, and beer and whisky as we men open up and start talking. It is amazing what a man does under these conditions.

He talks and talks. His heart opens up. This is where a man begins his journey into self-healing.

In November I was in New York and sitting in my deer stand at 7:30 in the morning when a six-point buck walked in front of me and stopped as though God placed him there. I was freezing and had a dose of buck fever so I was really shaking. I took aim and shot, a swing and a miss, so I took another and missed again. The deer flinched and walked away. Later that day on the evening hunt I saw a herd of does approach from left to right at sixty yards away. That time I used the BRAS technique of breathe, relax, aim, and squeeze the trigger, and I nailed one right in the heart. I was excited that I shot that well without a scope and using slugs. I hung up the deer and gutted her before carrying the carcass to the butcher for processing. We celebrated with a cigar and beer, as a man should. My heart comes alive in the adventure of the outdoors. I love watching outdoor hunting shows with my son, Jason, as he's become an avid fisherman and hunter. He shot his first buck in the fall of 2010 using a muzzle-loader with his grandpa. He is on his way to becoming a man.

Chapter 15

Forgiveness

I want to take some time and talk about forgiveness. On October 21, 2010, I was listening to a pastor in Chicago, Dr. James McDonald, from Walk in the Word Ministries. I learned that not forgiving is a cancer in the family. Get rid of it! Luke 6:37 says, *Judge not, and you shall not be judged. Condemn not, and you shall not be condemned. Forgive, and you will be forgiven.*

Forgiveness is a decision to release the person from the obligation. So what if the person does it repeatedly? As in Matthew 18:22, Jesus said to him, *"I do not say to you up to seven times, but up to seventy times seven."*

Here are some common excuses why we don't forgive. These are also known as dumb rationalization.

1. The hurt is too big
2. Time will heal it (and then we say time heals nothing).
3. I'll forgive when he or she says they are sorry.
4. I can't forgive if I can't forget.
5. If I forgive, they will just do it again.

The fallout is where you use revenge and this fills the heart with unforgiveness, which becomes the desire to see others suffer and make them feel what you have felt and are feeling. The fallout is huge by not letting go of wrong days.

Forgiveness has a direct and indirect improvement on the body and mind. Do not harbor resentment or anger. Positive emotions reduce your stress; you will become stable and relieve yourself of anxiety. Choose to sin, then choose to suffer. Jesus warns us against anything that gives a false sense of power.

A great question to ask yourself is "Where do I derive my strength from?" The world is screwed up. Let people feel the weight of who you are and let them deal with it. True masculinity is spiritual.

Joy

> *Therefore you now have sorrow; but I will see you again and your heart will rejoice, and your joy no one will take away from you.*
>
> —JOHN 16:22

The other big lesson learned from Dr. James McDonald Senior Pastor of Harvest Bible Chapel in Illinois and Joel Osteen well known Pastor of the Mega church in Houston, TX and author of many books. was on the topic of joy. So let's look at joy and what it does for you and what God says about joy.

Happiness is your choice and the result of that decision is a life that not only brings you days of joy but also brings joy to others through the contagious spirit of your smile and attitude.

As I was going through my worst experiences, I always knew through my faith that there was a reason why I was going through this. What was I to learn, what did I gain from this adversity? What I gained was the knowledge that after the darkness turns to light, I would be promoted to happiness. It's time to stop feeling bad and quit the self-pity. Instead start talking to yourself and say, "I am good. I do have what it takes, now and forever."

Put your hope in the Lord your God, like in Psalm 43:5: *Why are you cast down, O my soul? And why are you disquieted within me? Hope in God; For I shall yet praise Him, The help of my countenance and my God.*

Now it's time to stay positive and live each day full of joy.

> *…the voice of joy and the voice of gladness, the voice of the bridegroom and the voice of the bride, the voices of those who will say:*
>
> *"Praise the LORD of hosts, For the LORD is good, For His mercy endures forever."*
>
> *And of those who will bring the sacrifice of praise into the house of the LORD. For I will cause the captives of the land to return as at the first, says the LORD.*
>
> —JEREMIAH 33:11

In the above verse, God talks about how He will reverse this negativity you're in and restore you; this is an important part of building your positive and ever-joyous life to come. Life is full of disappointments: the bad economy, no job or just lost a job or not making enough money, the stock market not in your favor, and illness. You can see where I am going with this. Stop letting the circumstances around you control you.

Instead, take back control of your life. Learn how to cope with hardship or people stealing your joy; as these problems and people leave, others will replace them and new problems will replace past problems.

> But whatever house you enter, first say, "Peace to this house."
> And if a son of peace is there, your peace will rest on it; if not,
> it will return to you.
>
> —LUKE 10:5–6

This great verse talks about the exact thing. If the people you speak with do not accept your gift of peace, it's okay because that gift of peace will come back to you, anyway. This lesson was the hardest I had to learn, but the results are everlasting. I am at peace and feel God's love pouring over me in reward for the hard work I have put into myself for Him. In my view, Kate had a controlling personality once the children were born. She was also very negative in those last few years and I understand why, but still that's no excuse. She wore me out and beat me down, and that was when I checked out. I said to her on many occasions that I needed her to be more positive with me and quit tearing my spirit down in such a demeaning manner, especially in front of our children. I told her she had the tongue of a serpent that was vicious in attack. Yet she had no interest in curtailing her behavior. She became sarcastic and joked around, saying, "Hey honey, is this positive enough for you?"

At that moment I knew I needed out of such a negative environment that also was bringing down my children, before something happened that I would regret later. Once I took the power to control me and not her, my life started to change. She did not like losing her unbridled control and threw the relationship into a new dimension. Even after I left the house, she still tried her absolute best to control me through harsh arguing and telling me how to raise the children. As she heard I no longer spoke the way she did, she felt the control slip away. I was getting my power back, regaining strength and courage, and winning my life back. I have learned that you cannot fix another person, only yourself. When you put your energy into fixing someone else and always encouraging them, your energy is sapped right out and you wither away with them.

You will win your life back. Read God's Word and trust in Him with all your heart; He has you in the palm of His hand. You will win the greatest gift He has given, and that's your heart and life the way it was intended to be, to enjoy and love life not just endure and slug your way through it, and go through the motions of love. You have what it takes to reclaim your heart and soul and see the reward God has in store for you.

Chapter 16

An Eagle's Life

The bald eagle lives for about seventy years, but to reach this age, the eagle must make a hard decision. At forty, his long talons can no longer grab food and his long, sharp beak becomes bent. His aging wings grow heavy and stick to his chest, making it hard to fly. The eagle is left with the tough decision to die or go through a painful process that lasts 150 days. The eagle flies to the top of a mountain and sits on a nest. He knocks his beak against a rock until it falls out, and waits for a new beak to grow back to use in plucking out its overgrown talons. Once he has new talons, he thins out his feathers. After this five-month journey, he takes a flight of rebirth and lives for another thirty years. This story is a myth, but we can gain a much needed perspective from it as we must shed the past to rebuild our future and move forward. Like the eagle, we need change in our lives in order to grow.

In order to move forward we have to start the change process. We have to get rid of old memories and bad habits. Only when we are freed from these burdens can we take advantage of the present. Our lives are not determined by what happens but how we react—not by what life brings to us, but the attitude we bring to life.

A positive attitude causes a chain reaction of positive thoughts, events, and outcomes. It is a catalyst—the spark that creates extraordinary results. Believe and Action equals Results.

Most birds head for shelter when it rains. The eagle is the only bird that, to avoid the rain, flies above the clouds.

> *But those who wait on the LORD*
> *Shall renew their strength;*
> *They shall mount up with wings like eagles,*
> *They shall run and not be weary,*
> *They shall walk and not faint.*
>
> —ISAIAH 40:31

Chapter 17

That Empty
Home Feeling

M oving out of my apartment made for two moves in six months. It was a great feeling knowing I was leaving apartment living behind. Now the newest chapter of my journey began. I rented the house with four bedrooms and three and a half baths, on the water with a pool. Some might ask why I needed that much space. I wanted to make my children's lives as happy as I could, and the house was what I came up with. It was a newer home and very up-to-date in efficiency. For me it was serenity after months of noise. I also needed happiness because without myself happy I could not make my kids happy. If you have learned anything so far, it's about the children.

We have a life, too, and needs and wants, but you need to evaluate what's really important. To me, it's teaching my boys to become men; that's the chapter of life we are now on. I've learned through John Eldredge how important men are to their sons, and daughters, too.

That night after they left, I felt something different, called emptiness. I was not prepared for this hurdle or even saw it coming. I had an empty feeling, like, what am I doing here; this is a house for families, not just me. I sensed something missing and that was my wife. As night fell so did my heart, and I felt my true heart for the first time in a long time. I realized what a poser I had been. I would not hide from my true feelings anymore. It takes more energy to hide than to let them be.

A true heart is one free of resentment, unforgiveness, and pride. I hid behind the pride of saying she's not for me, she's not the one, she's whacko, she's…you get the point.

My true feelings at the time were that I missed her dearly. I wanted her in my life as my friend, soul mate, and lover. I wanted her to fill my emptiness. I started to think with my heart, not only my mind, and it said that after all that had happened between my wife and me, I still missed her. But remember, we were together almost nineteen years. The house stirred up the emotions, and I had to differentiate between what I thought I felt about her, and the addiction to our situation of many years together. I really just missed life. You are probably saying, *She treated you so badly in a negative way in the verbal and mental abuse department, how can you feel this way about her?* Simply, I let my heart answer not my brain, and it said, *Hang in there, and love for each other will find its way back into our hearts. I know I am in a different place than her right now, but that's okay. This is not a contest or a race, it's my life, and I have to do what's right for me in the pursuit for my heart and soul.* Looking deeper than ever into myself to renew my heart and make it a good and wise one took a lot of work and discipline during this time and maybe was part of the lesson God had given to me. It feels so good and right knowing that I can be a great husband to her or whoever God may put into my life. For me, getting over walking into an empty, quiet house in a different neighborhood was the next test in my journey. The next day the typical problems surfaced; the Internet and HDTV did not work. I called the cable provider and asked for them to send someone out, and they did the following day. The Internet and cable worked after a new high-definition box and modem from the local appliance store. It's amazing how we've become so dependent on technology. On my third day in the house, I went for my first bike ride in a week and it was great. Right from the front door, I started riding and put in thirty-five miles, which I was excited about.

Now I was able to get dressed and start riding from my front door. Sanity was a front door away. I was on to something; I felt joy and happiness being restored. So I decided to let my heart be known to Kate one last time. I dropped the kids off and said, *Okay, just let her know how you feel.* Men are built to be warriors and a warrior I am.

It took me a few minutes to speak without crying. Once I passed that stage, I spoke from my heart for the first time since I was single, and she wasn't ready. I said things like, "I miss you," "I love you," and "You're the missing link in my life and a void in the house even with the children." I did not want to confuse her any more than she was, only put my heart out there once again. She replied with "I can barely make it on what you are giving me and I need more and poor me because of this divorce you are forcing me to work, poor old me." Her self-pity began and she heard nothing from my heart.

The discussion with my wife was a dress rehearsal for the women I have in my life today, because God gave me the gift to recognize who will receive my true whole heart and hear it.

Since I left our house, not one bill has been late nor has she been unable to put gas in the car. All the essentials are taken care of. Above that, she needs to provide for herself. I also have my own rent and secondary child support, plus paying her attorney fees and mine, and other payments as I rebuild my life. So far she has had zero responsibility. I said, "Let's sit at the local courthouse and watch the people coming into the room and listen to their horrible stories, and see what's real in this world." She said, "We're different, Brian." I said we were not. We were getting divorced just like them.

The entire house had been remodeled so she has no capital expenditure for many years and she did not want to hear that. I am not sure what world she has been drawn into, but it's very dark, depressing, and miserable, from my view. Holding resentment and not forgiving allows your pride to get in the way of fixing your relationship. She holds all her pain against me 100 percent and feels totally cheated of a life in our marriage, and that's extremely dangerous. I forgive her daily and hold no resentment for the years we were together and the time we've been separated and now divorced.

Chapter 18

Life Restored

And God will wipe away every tear from their eyes; there shall be no more death, nor sorrow, nor crying. There shall be no more pain, for the former things have passed away.

Then He who sat on the throne said, "Behold, I make all things new." And he said to me, "Write, for these words are true and faithful."

—Revelation 21:4–5

A new life begins with the belief in Jesus Christ as it says in John 3:15, *That whoever believes in Him should not perish but have eternal life.* For those who want to start the journey to everlasting life, take a moment and with your heart say aloud this verse and you shall begin your new life with a new skin, and your journey into Christianity.

The above verses are powerful. Faith is the most important beginning to self-restoration as it will be your rock as you encounter the enemy, Satan, who wants to defeat you every chance he gets in your pursuit of the new you.

During self-evaluation, I have found music to be one of the best methods of meditation. Do not be disturbed or disappointed as you search for the new you. Look for signs and be careful of how you interpret them. Your heart and God will guide you to the right answer.

Things will be revealed to you because they are coming from your heart being restored. Think of this like a classic car in need of major restoration. Maybe it is as simple as wiping the oxidation off the headlight lens covers to make them look factory new. It's a process of taking away the old and making it new again. This process will be very hard for some and easy for others. It's all about you, so take your time and go at your own pace. I promise it will be worthwhile. As you go through your journey, you will see the woman you are with in a new light, one that you have never seen before, and now saying, who is this woman? The new you, the real you, the one God made, is coming forth. Always advance with caution to the woman you are separated from. Do not start by throwing your change into her face, but extend grace and let the bad things she said to you roll off as if you carried a shield.

Practice forgiveness when another person detonates negative words around you. You may have a relapse and be caught up in the battle again, but just pray for forgiveness for you and the other person with a repentant, whole heart. Now continue renewing your heart, which is the hardest part of the journey, where you encounter battle and want that instant healing power. Healing will come hourly, daily, and monthly. Stay on your course and do not allow anyone to derail your process. The distractions of the day will try to destroy joy, whether in the form of an argument or your spouse's attorney saying something to make you angry. That's exactly what the enemy wants to do: distract and derail you. Do not allow anyone or anything to forfeit your joy and new heart. When done daily, the process of letting go and forgiving will become a part of your life and a natural condition in your heart. All good things take time and effort, so stay with it and you will soon feel good.

It is up to you, with the free will God has given, to move as quickly as you want through this process. Don't allow things like not having enough time in the day. There are twenty-four hours in a day; you just have to find the time. I use my time alone to read the Bible and other books, not just self-help but even books on psychology to get a better understanding how we think from a psychological perspective. At times you will need to read books and watch movies that make you laugh. Your heart needs joy, so fill it with a good comedy or good book. Laughter and smiling are wellsprings of life. As you go through the process and start digesting this information, you need to process it at some time. Re-read certain books as you become clearer in your understanding of what is going on. The books will become so clear and you will devour them like you haven't eaten or drunk for years; that's it, you haven't. Now you see life through the eyes of your heart and a great scene is about to unfold. Reaffirm the positivity in your life and that you are good and have what it takes and you are on the right track.

Some great authors to read are Joel Hunter, senior pastor at Northland Church; John Eldredge of Ransomed Heart Ministries; Joel Osteen, pastor at Lakewood Church; and Dr. James Macdonald, pastor in Chicago. As your heart becomes new through forgiveness and repentance, your heart begins to see with new eyes and hear with new ears. You begin to feel and think with a good and wise heart for the first time.

Let's pray for the restoration of your heart and soul on this journey.

Lord,

What a great day as we ask for our hearts back. Father, please restore my soul and give my heart the wisdom to see Your Word and hear You as I learn to walk with You. I ask that I am healed from the past, and allowed to walk forward with a new heart that forgives the past seven times seventy, and is free of guilt. Father, a new life for me is a gift of grace and mercy that I ask for, will use this gift with the whole new heart that You are healing as I pray before You.

Restore me, Father, as I am ready to feel the wellspring of life flow through my veins. Lord Jesus, breathe new life into me and plant my feet on the rock, not the sand, through Your teachings. This will allow me to live my new life better than ever. Heal my heart, Jesus, as You have healed others and allow me to trust You and love You. You are the true Father, the one who will always love me no matter what. Jesus, forgive me, and all my sins. My heart is renewed as a whole, repentant heart, one that will love again and see life the way You intended it to be seen. Open the eyes of my heart, Lord, and let me see my new life unfold and live again, renewed in Jesus Christ.

Amen.

Where do we go from here? Great question. Start by reading the Bible and building the foundation of faith that is the foundation of the new you.

Look for friends that will help, not hinder you, that will listen to and support the new you, not the old you. Your transformation will let you see life like you never have before or not in a long time. You will rest at night as the yoke of unforgiveness, resentment, pride, and selfishness around your neck is chipped away. As your new heart and soul takes form you will hear and see with that new heart instead of just listening to what your mind says. Remember that the enemy, Satan, wants this to go away and will stop at nothing to win. Stand strong and believe in God and yourself. You are beautiful, and important to God the Father Almighty.

Chapter 19

Mediation

The day arrived for the mediation of my divorce. It was bittersweet for me. I had known this woman for nineteen years and it was going to be finished in a few hours. But I could finally get on with my life and leave the lawyers behind and start to put my new heart and soul to use.

The art of negotiating is a skill, so when considering a divorce attorney, ask how much they have mediated, and also how many trials they have conducted because this is where they earn their money. The rest is paperwork and the other party, generally the petitioner, is the one asking for everything and hoping for half. You need an attorney that sees through this and fights back now and then. Get yourself mentally prepared for the mediation process and write a list of your desires or the outcome you expect.

The four-hour period costs a lot of money, so stick to the facts and leave emotion out the best you can to keep down the cost. When deciding on the importance of issues, ask, how will this benefit my children or me?

Preparation is always important in divorce, especially mediation. Prepare as if it is an exam or an interview for a job. Research all you can; the knowledge gained will be an asset you can rely on. We don't plan to fail; we fail to plan. You might feel like going at your spouse with vengeance, but this is a great time to test your new heart. Understand the meaning of your new wise and good heart. Make informed choices and good decisions and you will come out on top. Don't allow your negative actions to get in the way of having a positive outcome. Stop the feelings of hate and bitterness and allow the positive flow you've worked so hard for to be revealed. Educate yourself in the idle months and prepare for the moment, and get ready to haggle as you would at a car dealership for a new car. The pressure will get high but stay grounded and calm and in control with a high degree of confidence.

When you feel overwhelmed, just breathe and look down at the list of desires or outcomes you wrote before entering the courtroom. Maybe include a quote that will allow you to snap out of it when needed.

When you feel "Oh, crap" and your brain is going to mush, read what you've written again. A great attorney who can recognize your fall and rescue you is very valuable. Do not be pressured to sign anything you do not want to, just for the sake of getting finished with the mediation. The lawyers will leave and go back to their lives and not care about your result or call to see how you are doing. Stay calm and breathe, and use all that you've rebuilt for this day. The warrior in you longs for battle and this may be the fight of a lifetime, so go in with the proper armor and sword and you will be fine. Let your lawyer do their job— that's what you pay them for—and when it's your turn to speak, do so.

Otherwise sit quiet and listen and take notes but do not confront the other attorney. Let yours do that.

If you have many assets, you stand to lose them; I can never underscore enough the need to educate yourself so your loss is as minimal as possible. You must get this right; this is the only shot you have in mediation before the court resolves the divorce.

The Day My Life Returns

Sleep was easy the night before mediation. Then morning came. It was scheduled at 9:00 a.m. on Thursday morning in one of the buildings lining downtown Orlando. I met my lawyer at 8:45, and at 9:00 we pushed the button on the elevator and waited for the doors to open. The ride seemed long and we stopped at the bankruptcy floor for a couple to get off the elevator. The doors closed and we began the ascent again. The doors opened and we entered the floor. Through the big glass doors, I could see my soon-to-be ex-wife sitting in the lobby corner to my right. She looked at me and smiled nervously. I didn't give her more than a glance.

When her attorney showed up, they entered the room together. The room was very bright as the big windows allowed for lots of light to enter. Just after 9:00 the mediator walked in and sat at the head of the boardroom table with his back facing the windows. He described the process and his background.

Then he asked that the petitioner go first with opening statements. As Kate's attorney delivered her statement, Kate's tears began to flow from across the table and I held mine back. The end was near and emotions started to surface. After that my attorney spoke and the mediator asked us to go into separate rooms, and this was when it began. After five and a half hours of negotiating at nine hundred dollars an hour, we were finished. The experience wasn't as draining as I thought it would be, but more of listening and staying calm and then delivering the best response that you could. I did successfully negotiate down from where we started. I had a paper binder to take notes and I looked at a page that had notes from a sermon I had listened to a week earlier by Dr. James McDonald about the book of Habakkuk. The sermon was on prayer and the levels of prayer request we go through from our beginning request to maturity.

The kindergarten level of prayer request is *Lord, give me this*; the high school level is *Lord, give me what I deserve*; and the college version is *Lord, don't give me what I deserve*. At the graduate school level the request is *Lord, I deserve nothing*.

I looked at these notes and read *I deserve nothing*. I stared out the huge window holding a cup of black coffee, and said, *Okay, God, I get it. I deserve nothing because better things are on the way.*

It was a humbling moment and I was ready to sign the agreement and move on, and receive the reward God had waiting for me. The next piece of the story comes from an e-mail of John Eldredge's daily reading. I read my e-mail to pass the time away as we waited for the mediator to come back after taking my offer to Kate. I read the daily reading and here is a part: *Faith looks back and draws courage; hope looks ahead and keeps desire alive.*

I read this and was floored.

The resurrection of our heart leads to the discovery of our role in the larger story. If we say we seek all this for our own sake, we are back where we started, lost in our own story. Jesus said that when a person lives merely to preserve his life, he eventually loses it.

Rather, He said, give your life away and discover life as it was meant to be. Self-help is no help at all. Self-sacrifice is the way to finding your true self. In Matthew 16:25, Jesus says, *For whoever desires to save his life will lose it, but whoever loses his life for My sake will find it.*

In another of John Eldredge's daily reading, he states that self-preservation is deeply wrong because it violates the Trinity, whose members live to bring glory to the others. The roads we travel will take us into battle to restore beauty in all things, chief among them the hearts of those we know. I read this and cannot believe what I am reading and how powerful it is to me at this time. As I read John Eldredge, it continues like this. We grow into glory so that we might assist others in doing so; we give our glory to increase theirs. In order to fulfill the purpose of our journey, we need a passion to increase glory; we need love.

After mediation I felt like I had given everything to her. Since God said I was doing the right thing, I wanted to know what was in this for me. I didn't understand. Was it once again to feel adversity and pain and learn to be humble and deny myself all? Then I read more of John Eldredge and he said memory, imagination, and a passion for glory must be kept close if we are to see the journey to its end. The road is not entirely rough; there are oases along the way. Thank God, I was thinking. It would be a dreadful mistake to assume that our Beloved is only waiting for us at the end of the road. Our communion with Him sustains us along our path.

I said to God, "I trust You. Now let's get down to the final mile, as I have been on this journey for seven months after leaving the house." I felt immediate relief and knew I was going to be okay and that my transformation was entering its final stage now. (Some of the above were excerpts from John Eldredge's *Sacred Romance: Drawing Closer to the Heart of God.*)

After the mediation was over, it felt like I had finished the seventh game of the Stanley Cup Finals, where we battled the entire game and check after check into the boards and the game was over a few brawls later. Then both teams lined up, shook hands, and said *Good game.* My now ex-wife Kate dashed out of the building without a look and I was left to say good-bye to the attorneys and mediators. I even went so far as to ask her attorney to buy us lunch, just to be a smart-ass. I had my parking ticket validated and the elevator quietly descended to the ground floor.

The doors opened and I walked to my car and drove away from the courthouse a divorced but happy, whole-hearted man. My journey has taken me a long way in seven months and now I begin a new chapter in a new life. So the question "Do I have what it takes?" has been answered and it is *yes*, a wholehearted yes.

Chapter 20

Where Do I Go from Here and Do I Have What It Takes?

These are great questions to ask yourself. Let me share this to help you get in the mindset for finding the answers.

> *Never sacrifice what you know is right for what is convenient or expedient. Live the life of a leader, one of values, character, courage, and commitment. What you do and tolerate in your presence demonstrates your standards. The prime measure of your standards is what you do when no one sees you doing it.*
>
> —AUTHOR UNKNOWN

Armed with the above and a new whole heart, meditate on your answers.

I will tell you that you do have what it takes, you will regain your soul and the heart of a warrior and restore your manhood, and that's where you go from here.

I told my story because I wanted to share how I have found life again after the trauma of divorce and give you a real view inside the life of divorce. I hope and pray that anyone reading this book sees they are good and worth it and they have what it takes. I promise that as you fight for your heart and soul, life will feel like it hasn't in a long time. You will see life in ways you have never considered, and your heart will speak to you and you will listen. Fight for your freedom and regain control of your life by showing the world you have arrived and you are the man, the warrior that God intended you to be.

About the
Author

B rian Nastovski is forty-five years old and a survivor of divorce with three beau-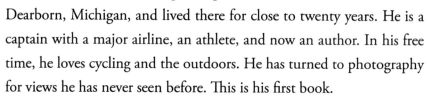tiful children. He is currently located in Orlando, Florida, where he has lived for the past twenty years. He grew up in Dearborn, Michigan, and lived there for close to twenty years. He is a captain with a major airline, an athlete, and now an author. In his free time, he loves cycling and the outdoors. He has turned to photography for views he has never seen before. This is his first book.

Conclusion

Congratulations as you embark on a life-changing event in reading this book and finding all the better in you. My hope is that my story helps you find your inner warrior spirit and you heal your heart as I did. It was my intention to share my story with you so that you know what the world of divorce is like and it either saves your marriage, if you're contemplating divorce, or it helps you get through one of the most ever challenging life events of your life. I did not write this book to talk negatively about my ex or use it as a "get even" tactic or even to bash divorce lawyers. When I decided to write this book I wanted to make sure it was a book my own kids could read and one that honors God. I also share with you the experience of divorce—its emotions and the process of mediation. It began as a healing process for me, and eventually I realized I needed to share what I have learned with other men who are hurting from divorce.

If you're contemplating divorce I have learned it can be beneficial to be the one filing. With planning and education you can make this experience less stressful than it can be. The other thing is the attorneys and courts make tons of cash at your expense. So have your story ready and get a great lawyer, one that you interview and you feel comfortable with using. Find one that likes to mediate and not go to court, which will save you thousands. Word of mouth is a start when looking for a lawyer, but at the end of the day it's how you feel with that office and their success in what it is your trying to achieve in your divorce.

In writing this book I pray that you do recapture your heart and soul so you may again live free after this rough time in your life. God puts us in situations that require trials so that we get to experience first-hand perseverance and character building skills and, most importantly, to come back to the Father Almighty for his comfort, wisdom, counsel, and trust. He wants us to give Him our problem, but to do this we first must trust Him and love Him with all our heart. He will then begin to heal us and return our heart to its wholeness. I will tell you that allowing no one to forfeit your new joy daily is one that takes lots of work and continuous practice, but ohhhhh is it worth it.

You reading this book is just one of the many steps that will help you achieve that whole-heart loving feeling and I will be with you every step of the way. I want you to leave this book motivated, encouraged, and knowing God has a bigger plan for you and that the best in you is yet to come. I also shared with you what I feel a great marriage should be like as it is with my sincere hope that you will give marriage another shot and it will be the one that lasts for eternity. If you're early on in the stage of contemplating divorce, then I pray that this book finds you and regroups you and brings your marriage back to life in a way that will make everyone around you proud and make the Father Almighty smile with pleasure in your accomplishment.

After reading this book, I ask that you please take the time to get your heart and mind right with God then you will totally reap the benefits of what I talked about. I want you to know you have what it takes and you are a winner. You will stand victorious and God will renew your days so that you may have the best years ahead of you.

God will either renew your current relationship or open the doors to a new and ever-loving one soon.

Take this opportunity to also renew the time you spend with your kids. Enjoy them as you never have before. Engage with them by listening to them and understanding how they feel, and just watch them as you are building the best memories ever. You will begin to see them in a different light and those things that may have once bothered you no longer will. It's called the healing heart and soul and it will change your whole perspective on life.

God is great and He is about to change your life forever, so open your heart now to Him and allow His Holy Spirit to infuse you with His love.

The love you have toward God is the way you will begin to love others again so wholeheartedly. Now I ask that you *just breathe* because God has your back. Let this book inspire and encourage you to be more than you are today and to become that awesome man everyone will look up and say, I want what you have. God has opened the door; now just walk in and embrace Him.

As you change your heart, you will change and experience the life God intended for you. He knows everything about you so don't hide, just let all your problems go to Him. Be as transparent as you have ever been and ask for God's favor now. He is listening and knows what you're going to say before you say it. So come now and Praise the Holy Father, worship Him and give thanks for all now and what is to come.

Let us pray for your heart now:

> *Lord,*
>
> *I come before you and ask that you set these men free of all bondage and forgive them Father as they ask for your forgiveness with an open heart for their past. Lord, open the eyes of their hearts and with their new eyes see your word and hear you with their new heart. Make their hearts new and bring forth the warrior spirit in them. Show them their masculine hearts and teach them wisdom and bring them back from a dead heart and open the wellspring of life in them. Lord. I ask that you start to heal their wounded and broken hearts. Heal them from all the past they may be holding on to and give them a heart free from resentment, guilt, and un-forgiveness and pride. I ask that you give them the strength to fight onward in their journey toward the masculine heart that they long for. I ask that you arm them with the breast plate of righteousness, gird their waist with truth,*

give them the shield of faith, and shod their feet with the gospel of peace. Please equip them with the helmet of salvation and sword of the Spirit that is your word Lord. Lord pour out your love for them and allow them to renew their hearts to love you and trust you as they have never before. Father, invoke their warrior spirit as you are a warrior, one that fights for us daily. I ask that you bless each and every one of them in the name of Jesus Christ.

    AMEN

CPSIA information can be obtained at www.ICGtesting.com
Printed in the USA
BVOW080301220413

318721BV00001B/3/P